THE POCKET IDIOT'S GUIDE™ TO

Texas Hold'em

Second Edition

by Randy Burgess and Carl Baldassarre

ALPHA

A member of Penguin Group (USA) Inc.

ALPHA BOOKS

Published by the Penguin Group

Penguin Group (USA) Inc., 375 Hudson Street, New York, New York 10014, U.S.A.

Penguin Group (Canada), 10 Alcorn Avenue, Toronto, Ontario, Canada M4V 3B2 (a division of Pearson Penguin Canada Inc.)

Penguin Books Ltd, 80 Strand, London WC2R 0RL, England

Penguin Ireland, 25 St Stephen's Green, Dublin 2, Ireland (a division of Penguin Books Ltd)

Penguin Group (Australia), 250 Camberwell Road, Camberwell, Victoria 3124, Australia (a division of Pearson Australia Group Pty Ltd)

Penguin Books India Pvt Ltd, 11 Community Centre, Panchsheel Park, New Delhi—110 017, India

Penguin Group (NZ), cnr Airborne and Rosedale Roads, Albany, Auckland 1310, New Zealand (a division of Pearson New Zealand Ltd)

Penguin Books (South Africa) (Pty) Ltd, 24 Sturdee Avenue, Rosebank, Johannesburg 2196, South Africa

Penguin Books Ltd, Registered Offices: 80 Strand, London WC2R 0RL, England

International Standard Book Number: 1-59257-563-3
Library of Congress Catalog Card Number: 2006924292

08   8 7 6 5 4 3

Interpretation of the printing code: The rightmost number of the first series of numbers is the year of the book's printing; the rightmost number of the second series of numbers is the number of the book's printing. For example, a printing code of 06-1 shows that the first printing occurred in 2006.

Printed in the United States of America

Note: This publication contains the opinions and ideas of its authors. It is intended to provide helpful and informative material on the subject matter covered. It is sold with the understanding that the authors and publisher are not engaged in rendering professional services in the book. If the reader requires personal assistance or advice, a competent professional should be consulted.

The authors and publisher specifically disclaim any responsibility for any liabil-ity, loss, or risk, personal or otherwise, which is incurred as a consequence, directly or indirectly, of the use and application of any of the contents of this book.

Contents

Introduction

Hold'em poker is America's game. It's the game of the World Series of Poker in Las Vegas, and the game friends choose to play around the kitchen table. Now you can make it your game.

This guide teaches you everything you need to know to play Hold'em. And not just how to play, but how to win. We've never played with anyone who doesn't like winning, so we're going to assume you'll enjoy it, too.

There's plenty to know about Hold'em, but learning how to play the game well isn't a subject reserved for cigar-smoking Texans or stone-faced young men in wraparound sunglasses. Hold'em is a great equalizer. In a home game, a computer technician can take a CEO's money. In the casino, a 65-year-old grandmother can outplay a flashy young gambler. All it takes is a little study, and you can stretch your entertainment dollar much farther than with house games such as roulette or craps, where you're guaranteed to lose.

And when we say "a little study," that's exactly what we mean: no matter what the topic, we've kept our explanations simple. This applies not only to basic information such as the rules of the game, but also to advanced topics such as playing multiple tables on the Internet or categorizing opponents by playing style.

Another feature of this expanded second edition is not just one, but *two* chapters on no-limit Hold'em: first, a primer on the basics, and second, a condensed but tip-packed guide to no-limit tournaments. We hope to not only whet your appetite for this popular form of Hold'em, but to get you well started.

Finally, whatever form of Hold'em you play, you'll find that many of your opponents won't have taken the time to read a book like this. We guarantee you an advantage over them, even if you've never played before in your life.

Extras

In addition to the main text, this book includes sidebars, each with a distinctive visual cue:

Talk Like a Texan _____

These sidebars include definitions of basic Hold'em terms.

Build Your Stack _____

These provide insights and side glimpses into poker lore and poker fact.

Raise It Up

These are playing tips that show you how to strategize and win.

Watch Your Chips

These warnings tell you what to watch out for and how to avoid common mistakes.

We've also sprinkled quizzes throughout the book. Take these quizzes seriously. For example, cover up the answers and think about the questions before you read the answers—you'll learn Hold'em even faster.

Acknowledgments

Both of us are grateful to Joe Bunevith, a.k.a. Joe Tall, for taking time away from the tables to review the strategy portions of this book. We also thank Thom Forbes, home-game honcho extraordinaire; Mike Sanders of Alpha Books; and our agent, Bob Diforio, for dealing us in on this project.

In addition, Carl thanks Randy, his co-author, for being a good Hold'em player, a great writer, and an even better friend; Marian, his wife, for her love, spirit, and extraordinary generosity in putting up with late nights spent playing Hold'em, and still more late nights writing about it; and Marie, Juliana, and Justin, my set of aces.

Randy for his part admits that Carl, too, may be a good writer and friend—but what about all those leaks in his Hold'em game? Never mind that Carl's lifetime winnings are far bigger than Randy's. That's just variance!

On a somewhat more gracious note, Randy also thanks Katherine, Bob, and Celeste: the best part of poker is being able to leave the table and come back home to them.

Trademarks

Sit On Down, Pardner

In This Chapter

- Why play Hold'em?
- Where to find games
- Hold'em myths versus the real deal
- How to achieve your goals

Corky McQuorcodale, a traveling poker player, is widely credited with having brought a new form of poker to Las Vegas in 1963. Known as Texas Hold'em—or just plain Hold'em—the game's popularity spread over the next four decades.

Now it's not only the most popular form of poker in the world, it's the most popular of *all time*. As you read this, millions are playing it in casinos, clubs, home games, and on the Internet. And the odds are, you picked up this book because you play Hold'em already and want to improve, or you want to learn how to get started.

Whether you're into the game or still undecided, in this chapter, we'll put all the cards on the table and take a look at the forces behind the Texas Hold'em boom.

Why Play Hold'em?

Of course, you have your own good reasons for wanting to learn Hold'em, but there could be a couple more that you haven't thought of. This section describes four of the best, as we see them.

Reason 1: It's Fun

Hey, it's a game! If you enjoy board or card games, you'll probably like Hold'em. And there are additional pleasures, depending on your setting. If you're playing a good home game, the insults, banter, and sociability can be as entertaining as the cards. In a casino, you can enjoy the swank feel of genuine green felt, the hefty, custom-designed clay chips, and the luxury of ordering food or drink without leaving your seat.

Reason 2: It's Easy

Even if you've never played Hold'em before, you can get started in just a few minutes. Chapter 2 explains the rules quickly and simply. Read it, deal out a few practice hands, review the strategy tips in the rest of this book, and you'll be ready to play.

Build Your Stack

Texas Hold'em may not have even originated in Texas! Early forms of poker, based on century-old European card games, were first played in New Orleans in the early 1800s. As poker moved northward on the Mississippi with riverboat gamblers, draw, five-card stud, and seven-card stud emerged as popular variations. Hold'em didn't even originate until sometime around 1900, poker historians speculate. Why it remained largely unknown for so long is still a mystery.

Reason 3: It's Challenging

This may sound like a direct contradiction to Reason 2, but rest assured it isn't. Although the basics of Hold'em are easy to learn, playing at a high level can take years of thought and study.

According to experts in both games, Hold'em and bridge are comparable in difficulty. Some even say Hold'em is as demanding as chess. (In fact, many young American masters these days also play Hold'em!)

However, mastery of Hold'em requires a different combination of skills than other games. The best players rely on a unique combination of mathematics, psychology, and card sense.

Finally, Hold'em is challenging because you can keep raising the stakes. At each higher level, both the pressure and the relative skill of your opponents increase, too. After all, it's a lot different playing for millions of dollars in a nationally televised tournament than playing for quarters around the kitchen table.

This is to your advantage. When you're starting out, you can find a level of play that you're comfortable with and stick with it as long as you like. There's no pressure, and if you start to get bored, you can always find some new and interesting aspect of the game to work on. Any time you want to move up to more challenging levels and stakes, new games and players will be waiting for you.

Reason 4: It Can Make You Money

If you play Hold'em regularly, you'll encounter fellow players who treat poker as if luck determines all, just as it does in casino games like roulette, craps, or keno.

They're wrong. As of now, you are officially on notice: winning at Hold'em over the long run is a matter of skill, not luck. That's why there are professional players in poker, but not roulette.

The great majority of Hold'em players lose money no matter how long they play. Though exact figures are not available, it's our guess that thousands of players make a living at this game. In addition, a greater number rely on their winnings to supplement income from other sources.

This guide can help you become one of the winners. But this doesn't mean that making a buck should be your primary reason to learn the game. Unless you turn out to be a poker prodigy, the time you invest in the game might be more profitably spent working or developing marketable skills for use outside the world of poker.

Still, a hobby that could potentially pay for itself is a pretty good deal. And the excitement of winning can be just as great, even when the amounts involved are small.

Raise It Up

Just how often can a good player win at Hold'em? Excluding tournaments and no-limit Hold'em, a common benchmark is one bet per hour. So if you're playing in a casino or club game where the top bet is $4, you'd be doing well to average that much for each hour of play. Really strong players target 1.5 bets per hour. Online, where play is faster, winning between two and three bets for every 100 hands is roughly comparable.

Places to Play

Hold'em has never been more popular than it is right now. When you're ready to play, you can find a game in plenty of places. Here's a quick look at the pros and cons of your main choices.

Home Games

Most people first learn to play poker in home games. It's hard to beat the relaxed pace of play, the small stakes, and the chance to socialize and learn with friends.

Many home games are "dealer's choice." That means it's likely you'll play some Hold'em along with other forms of poker, like seven-card stud, Omaha, or draw. Some players may want to include wildcard games or other exotic variants.

To keep the games friendly, many home games deliberately keep the stakes low. Although good for sociability, this also encourages players to stay in for nearly every hand. This can keep you from learning the tactics necessary for winning in games that are even slightly less congenial.

If you're serious about playing well, you'll probably be a consistent winner. After awhile, you may want to hone your skills against other serious players. If so, we suggest you look for a casino, cardroom, or Internet poker site. You can still play in your friendly home game when you're in the mood.

Casinos

Casinos are a great place to learn Hold'em. Many have a separate poker room, whether it's an actual room or a section of the main floor, populated by table after table of experienced players. Don't let that intimidate you. Welcoming newcomers is good business, so some casinos offer practice tables and most have plenty of low-stakes tables. Although the game may seem confusing during your first few games, most dealers are patient with new players. With the growing popularity of the game, it's unlikely you'll be the only beginner. It also helps to remember that if the regulars at your table were all that good, they'd have moved up to bigger stakes long ago.

 Build Your Stack

> One tip: many casinos don't offer poker of any kind. To avoid disappointment, call ahead about having a poker room and ask if they spread Hold'em at stakes you're comfortable with.

Cardrooms and Clubs

A large cardroom offers an experience similar to a casino. The biggest difference is that cardrooms typically have fewer nonpoker games than casinos. Some have only poker, while others sustain other card games as well.

Cardrooms are common in some states, notably California. Their size ranges from immense "card barns" with dozens of tables to tiny, single-table establishments.

In places where cardrooms aren't legal, underground poker clubs often spring up. The movie *Rounders* depicted several fictitious clubs in New York City.

Although the clubs in that movie were dramatic and menacing, real illegal clubs can be safe and pleasant places to play, much like chess, bridge, or backgammon clubs. If you play in an area where such clubs exist, you'll probably hear about one at some point. If you decide to go, be aware that there's a chance the club could be raided by police. In most states, playing isn't against the law, so only the club operators and employees are subject to arrest. But you should check the law in your area before you play. If there ever *were* a police raid, your chips would likely be confiscated as evidence. It's also probably wise to bring a friend the first time you visit, and be ready to leave if anything about the club or the other players makes you uncomfortable.

The Internet

Cyberspace is currently the most popular place to play Hold'em. On a single night, more than 80,000 cardsharks can gather for Hold'em at one of the more popular Internet sites. No casino or cardroom in the world can come close to matching those staggering numbers. And remember, that's just one site of dozens.

Of course, many people love the sociability of a live game and the feel of real cards and chips. But many others prefer the convenience of having a game available wherever there's a computer and an Internet connection. For those who don't live near a place to play, the Internet offers the only game in town.

There are many reasons to like online poker, especially if you're a beginner. For one thing, the online poker sites have low overhead, so they can offer *much* lower stakes than you'll find anywhere else. It's commonplace to find Hold'em games where the maximum bet is 25¢ or 50¢, for example. Many sites also offer "play money" games, if you want to get your feet wet without risking even a mild soaking.

Online play allows you to learn the game at an accelerated pace. In a casino you might see 35 hands an hour, whereas online you'll typically see at least 70. So if you're comfortable using a computer, you get twice as many chances per hour to improve your game.

Having listed the advantages of Internet Hold'em, we'd be remiss if we didn't mention one potential drawback: running an Internet poker site is illegal in the United States. All the major sites are based offshore.

With advertisements on television and on the Internet, the big poker sites certainly aren't hiding what they're doing. Neither are many players— people continue to play openly in homes, offices, and Internet cafes. Although attempts to regulate the free-wheeling world of Internet poker are in the works as of this writing, most players appear to be simply ignoring the issue at present.

> **Watch Your Chips**
>
> Poker is a social game—and yet you'll often hear players complain about their luck, berate the dealer, or criticize their opponents for making "stupid" plays. Smart players don't act this way, and you shouldn't either. Channel your aggressive instincts into playing your hardest, not taking a hard-nosed attitude. You'll have a better time, and you'll probably play better if you're not distracted by frustration or anger.

Make-Believe Versus the Real Deal

We've already touched on one of the most common misconceptions about Hold'em—the notion that luck trumps skill. If most of your poker experience has been watching movies such as *Rounders* or televised tournaments such as the World Series of Poker, you may have a few other misguided notions, too. Let's debunk these before going any further to make sure they don't cost you bets at the table.

- **Make-Believe: Hold'em is an action game where you play lots of hands.** The dealer pitches the cards, the camera zooms in, and the chips start to fly. What else is there?

The Real Deal: Hold'em involves a lot of sitting and waiting. It's not exciting and the cameras don't dwell on it, but a good Hold'em player spends far more time folding his first two cards than playing them. This is true even in tournaments, where various gimmicks such as stack-devouring antes force you to play many more hands than normal. As you'll find out in the next few chapters, it pays to be picky.

- **Make-Believe: You have to bluff a lot.** In both movies and televised tournaments, the combatants frequently win huge pots with bold bluffs. Even though you're just starting out, you may be thinking you can do the same.

  The Real Deal: At low limits, you should rarely bluff. Those big bluffers are playing no-limit Hold'em, where a good bluff can sometimes steal a huge pot. However, most of this book is about playing limit Hold'em, where the small bet size means that bluffs are usually called and the best hand takes the pot. We'll talk about bluffing in the chapters on no-limit, tournaments, and advanced play. But for now, suffice it to say that bluffing is much less important than people think.

- **Make-Believe: You'll often have to out-play a single opponent.** Just as in *Rounders*, you and John Malkovich head-up, right?

> **The Real Deal: You'll usually have many opponents.** Put your Matt Damonesque fantasies aside: at many low-limit Hold'em tables, it's common to reach the showdown with several opponents, with only an occasional head-up confrontation. You'll rely less on bluffing than on playing strategies that do well against a crowd.

Setting Your Sights

So why exactly *do* people play Hold'em? We went over the reasons before, but this section describes a few real-life examples.

One player is an engineer at a large company who plays Hold'em more than 25 hours a week. He's a former college athlete, very competitive, and regularly plays for big stakes in games that often include professional players. His main goals are to constantly improve his game and to win money to supplement his income.

Another player successfully freelances as a writer. He's a consistent winner in low-stakes games, even though work and a growing family allow him time to play only a few hours a week. His main goals are to pursue an enjoyable hobby while slowly building his skills and his winnings.

Finally, we have one player who is a highly successful software executive who occasionally takes time away from the office to play low-stakes Hold'em.

Reports suggest he probably doesn't play enough to be a consistent winner, but we doubt he minds losing a few dollars. That man is Bill Gates, the founder of Microsoft. We have no way of knowing for sure, but we'd guess his goal might be simply to spend a few hours relaxing.

Now it's your turn. Before you invest any more time or money in the game, decide what you want to receive in return. Relaxation? Money? Sociability? Competition? Mental stimulation? Winning the World Series of Poker?

By setting goals from the start, you'll create a way to assess how you're doing as your Hold'em game evolves and improves.

The Least You Need to Know

- Hold'em is a form of poker that's recently become the most popular variation of the game.
- Skill is more important than luck. In the long run, a good player can expect to be an overall winner.
- You can play Hold'em at home with friends, in casinos and cardrooms, and on the Internet.
- Luck, bluffing, and fancy one-on-one moves are much less important than most new Hold'em players think.

Hold'em Basics

In This Chapter

- Ranking of hands
- Dealing Hold'em
- Learning how betting works
- Reading the board and examples

Before you begin learning the strategies and tactics that make winning Hold'em so much fun, you need to know the absolute basics. By the end of this chapter, you'll understand how the cards are dealt, how the betting works, and a little bit more besides. We're not talking mastery here, just enough to get you started.

First, let's make sure you're ready. If you haven't played a lick of poker in your life, you'll need to acquaint yourself with the most fundamental poker concept of all—what makes a winning hand. If you already know this, you can skip ahead.

Five might be the most important number in poker, if only because five cards make a complete poker hand. This is true no matter how many cards you're dealt, whether seven, as in seven-card-stud, or just two, as in Hold'em. (Hmm, how can you make a five-card hand if you're only dealt two cards? We'll solve that mystery in a page or two.)

This leads us to our next topic: the ranking of the different possible hands. Not coincidentally, they're ranked by how often they occur. Hard-to-get hands are top dog, while everyday mongrels command little respect. For example, if you deal out five-card hands to yourself from a shuffled deck, you'll average getting a pair every other hand. By contrast, three-of-a-kind will come along just once every 34 hands. Take a gander at the table and then let's talk about it.

You'll see that in Hold'em poker, a Ten is abbreviated not as 10, but as T. More obviously, an Ace is abbreviated as A, a King as K, and so on for the face cards. Cards from 9 down are simply referred to by number. We'll talk about additional abbreviations in Chapter 4.

Rank of Poker Hands

Name	Examples	Ways to Get This Hand	Odds Against If Dealt 5 Cards
Royal flush	A♦ K♦ Q♦ J♦ T♦	4	649,739 to 1
Straight flush	8♠ 7♠ 6♠ 5♠ 4♠	36	64,973 to 1
Four of a kind	7 7 7 7 5	624	3,913 to 1
Full house	3 3 3 K K	3,744	589 to 1
Flush	J♥ 9♥ 5♥ 4♥ 2♥	5,108	272 to 1
Straight	J T 9 8 7	10,200	131 to 1
Three of a kind	8 8 8 A K	54,912	34 to 1
Two pair	7 7 6 6 Q	123,552	12 to 1
One pair	J J A 9 3	1,098,240	Even
No pair	K T 9 8 7	1,302,540	

Here are some fine points on determining the *best hand*:

- **If more than one player has a full house,** the highest ranking three-of-a-kind wins. For example, QQQ 22 beats 444 AA.

- **Between competing flushes or competing straights,** the high card determines the winner: for example, a Jack-high straight beats a Ten-high straight. The highest possible straight is Ten through Ace; the smallest possible straight is Ace through Five, with the Ace counting as the lowest card, rather than the highest. (In poker parlance, this kind of straight is often called a *wheel* or a *bicycle*.) And no, you can't make an "around-the-corner" straight by going from low to high—for example, QKA23.

  For flushes only, if the top card is a tie, the next card counts, and so on down to the last card: for example, AQ983 beats AQ982.

- **If more than one player has two pair,** the highest pair wins. For example, AA 22 beats KK QQ. If two players have the same two pair, then the fifth card counts: AA 22 5 beats AA 22 3.

- **If nobody has a pair,** the winner is the player holding the highest card. If there's a tie, you can go all the way down to the last card, just as with two battling flushes.

- **In the case of a tie in every respect,** the players split the pot.

Raise It Up

As you learn the ranking of the hands, remember that a small hand such as an Ace-high can win a lot of money if it's the **best hand** at the time. And a big hand such as a straight flush may win only peanuts if no other big hands are around to contest it. Always remember, value in poker is relative, not absolute.

Dealing the Cards

To start with, each player is dealt two cards face down. These cards are known as _hole cards_, and in Hold'em, they're the only cards that are yours alone. A round of betting follows. Next, the dealer _burns_ the top card in the deck—that is, he discards it sight-unseen, face down on the table. Now he deals three cards face up in the center of the table. This is the _flop_. These three cards are community cards, meaning everyone can use them. There's another round of betting.

The dealer now deals a fourth face-up card, called the _turn_. Again, it's a shared card that all players can use, and again, it's followed by a round of betting. A fifth and final card is dealt face-up, called the _river_. There's one last round of betting. If more than one player is left in the hand, there's a showdown: the players flip over their hole cards to see who has the best hand. The five cards in the middle are collectively called the *board*. Each player gets to combine one, both, or none of his hole cards with any of the cards from the board to create his best five-card poker hand.

 Talk Like a Texan

> To **burn** means to discard the top card from the deck, face down. In Hold'em, the dealer does this before dealing the flop, the turn, and the river. Why? Ostensibly, it's to prevent cheating—for example, if any of the cards have been marked or scuffed in a way that makes them identifiable. Although such caution is usually unnecessary, burning is a hallowed Hold'em tradition.

You Can't Bet the Moon

Let's turn our attention to the essence of poker—betting. The first thing to know is how *much* you can bet. The answer isn't "how thick is your wallet?" but "what's the betting structure?" There are four basic structures:

- **No-limit.** This is what they play in the Main Event at the World Series of Poker. You can bet just one chip or your entire stack of chips at any point in the hand. We'll talk more about this in Chapter 9.

- **Pot-limit.** The pot is the money in the middle of the table—so when we say pot-limit, it means you can bet or raise any amount up to the total amount in the pot. Like no-limit, pot-limit is a game for experienced players.

- **Spread-limit.** Limit poker means exactly that: bets and raises are limited to a set amount, generally smaller than the pot. In spread-limit, you can bet or raise any amount between a minimum and maximum. For example, in $1–$3 spread-limit, a common beginner game at many casinos, you can bet anywhere from $1 to $3 at any time. The only qualification is that a raise must be at least as big as the preceding bet.

- **Structured-limit.** This is the most common betting structure outside of tournaments, and the one we'll be referring to most often in this book. Bets before the flop and on the flop are one amount, and bets on the turn and river are exactly double this amount. For example, in $3/$6 structured-limit, bets or raises before the flop and on the flop are $3, and bets and raises on the turn and river are $6.

Betting Blind

While we're on the subject of betting, remember that all forms of poker require some money go into the pot before any cards are dealt. Otherwise there'd be nothing to play for and everyone would sit tight until they got perfect cards.

Games such as seven-card stud or five-card draw seed the pot by requiring each player to contribute a fraction of a bet, called an *ante*. Hold'em is also played this way in some home games.

Casinos or clubs, however, use a different method for Hold'em: two players are required to contribute blind bets to the pot, or *blinds*. In a limit game, the player who is the *big blind* must contribute a bet equal to the limit, while the *little blind* must contribute either ⅓, ½, or ⅔ of a bet.

Obviously it's a handicap to have to put money into the pot without seeing your cards first. To ensure everyone takes their turn, a plastic disc that looks a little like a white hockey puck is moved clockwise around the table, one position with each deal. This disk is called the *dealer button*. The player who has the button is called either the *button*, or the *dealer*, regardless of the fact that there's a professional dealer doing the actual handing out of cards.

The little blind sits to the immediate left of the dealer button, and the big blind sits two seats to the left. This way everyone pays his or her dues as big and little blind, and everyone gets a chance to be dealer.

Putting Cards and Betting Together

You're just about ready to play some sample hands. But first, let's look at how the cards, the blinds, and the betting work together.

Before the Flop

Before any cards are dealt, the big and little blinds put forward their blind bets. It's proper etiquette to place these chips in front of you, rather than toss them directly into the pot. The dealer will gather them up after the betting is done for the round.

Now the dealer gives everyone his or her hole cards. These are yours alone to look at, and it actually matters how you go about this. To avoid flashing a card, seasoned Hold'em players never pick the hole cards up off the table. Instead, bring your two cards neatly together, still face down, then cup your hands over them and use a thumb to peel up the ends nearest you—just enough so that you and only you can see what you've got.

Betting begins with the player seated to the immediate left of the big blind, or *under the gun*. This player can *call* the blind bet by placing chips to match in front of him, or *fold*, in which case he surrenders his cards by pushing them face down toward the dealer. If he likes his hand, however, he can also *raise*. For example, in a $3/$6 structured-limit game, he could raise the big blind's $3 bet by another $3, making the total bet $6.

> ### Watch Your Chips
>
> There's a rule in clubs and casinos that if you don't protect your hole cards, they can be rendered unplayable if another player throws away his or her cards and those cards touch yours. You can also lose your cards if the dealer accidentally gathers them as he's collecting other players' folded hands. Fortunately, protecting your hand is easy: after you've looked at your cards, and hopefully memorized them, place a chip or a coin on top of them.

The betting continues clockwise. Each player in turn chooses to call, fold, or raise. In most games, the number of raises is limited to three or four per betting round. The exception is when only two players are involved, in which case casinos and clubs usually permit an unlimited number of raises.

When the action gets around to the little blind, she, too, must call, fold, or raise. In any case, she has already paid a fraction of a bet, so it's cheaper for her to call than for the other players. If she folds, she forfeits her blind.

The big blind is last to act before the flop. He's got the same options as the players before him, with one difference: because he's already put in a full bet, he can simply check, indicating he's taking no further action, if no one has raised and he himself doesn't want to raise. He does this either by saying "check" or by rapping the table.

Raise It Up _____

If you've got the dealer button before the flop and everyone in front of you folds, you can consider raising even with mediocre cards. Your goal is to "steal" the blinds, by folding all the remaining players.

Occasionally everyone will fold to the little blind. In that case the big blind and little blind can either play it out, or else agree to take back their blinds. The latter practice is known as **chopping,** and it can save you from being penalized by the ominous-sounding *rake*. For more on the rake, see Chapter 7.

On the Flop

After the three common cards of the flop are dealt, betting starts again. This time, whoever is immediately to the left of the dealer leads off. If the little blind called the bet before the flop, this will be her. Because in this round no one has bet yet, she has the option of checking, meaning she takes no action or betting.

The betting action keeps moving to the left. If the first player checked, the next player has the same options of either checking or betting. But if the first player bet, the next player must now either call that bet, fold, or raise.

The action continues around the table, until either everyone has checked, or someone has opened the betting and gotten at least one caller (or possibly a raiser). If everyone checks, then everyone remains in and gets to see the turn card. But if someone bets, only those players who call that bet (or raise it) get to see the turn card. Otherwise they must fold. If no one calls, the bettor wins the pot automatically.

Of course, after someone puts in the first bet, all other players are free to not merely call but raise, with additional raises possible after that, until the maximum of three or four has been reached. Once again, there must be at least one caller of a raise or reraise for the action to proceed to the next stage. If not, the raiser or reraiser wins the pot right there.

On the Turn and River

Betting on the turn and the river is just like betting on the flop. In each case, the first remaining player to the left of the dealer button is first to act.

On the river, if more than one player is left in the hand after the betting is over, the players flip over their hands. This is called the *showdown*. The dealer pushes the pot to the winner, or if there's a tie, he splits the pot accordingly. The button is moved one *position* to the left, the dealer shuffles the cards, and it starts all over again.

Raise It Up

You may have noticed that the player with the dealer button gets to act last on the flop, turn, and river. If that seems like an advantage, congratulations, you're on your way to becoming a winning Hold'em player!

Being last to act is called having **position**, and is indeed an edge. You get to see what everyone else does and act accordingly, while they can only guess at what you'll do. We'll talk more about the importance of position in further chapters.

Let's Play!

We're ready for our example hands. You can just read along, but it wouldn't hurt to get out a deck of cards and deal them out to match the example. It's like learning to speak a foreign language—the more realistic you can make it, the faster it'll sink in.

Example One

Hold'em can be played with as few as two players, in which case we say they're playing *head-up* or *heads-up*, to as many as 10, which we call a *ring game*.

To keep things simple for our example, we'll have just four players: Larry, Moe, Joe, and Sally. This is sometimes called a *shorthanded game*, as compared to a ring game.

Let's get to our action.

Preflop

Sally had the dealer button for the hand before, so now it slides over to Larry. It's a $3/$6 limit game, so Moe posts a little blind of $1, and Joe posts a big blind of $3. Now the players get their cards.

Remember that before the flop, it's not the big and little blind who act first, but the player who is to their immediate left—the player under the gun. In this case, it's Sally. She loves her Ace-King combo. It's a powerful hand, so she raises, putting forward $6 in chips.

Larry takes one look at the dreck he's been dealt and *mucks* it, pushing the cards face down toward the dealer. He'll rarely win a pot with Q8 offsuit (unsuited), so he's better off just watching.

Moe and Joe have decent hands, however, so they both call the raise. Moe puts in $5 in addition to his $1 blind, and Joe puts in $3.

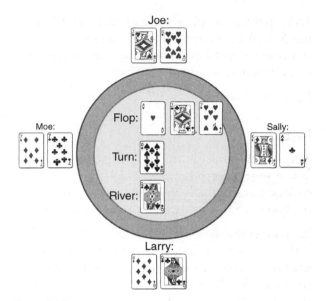

Example One

Flop

Stop! Before you read on, stop and look at the table, then work out for yourself what each active player now holds for his or her best five-card poker hand.

Ready? Let's resume the action.

Moe, the little blind, is excited: he's flopped what in Hold'em parlance is called a *set*—three-of-a-kind, with two of the three cards being his hole cards. This is a very powerful hand, so Moe unhesitatingly bets the limit of $3.

Joe, the big blind, likes his hand, too, so he calls the bet. He's flopped *second pair*, meaning the second-best possible pair hand, with his pair of Jacks. In addition, he has a flush *draw*—either of the two cards to come can give him a flush in Hearts. Stop and work it out if you don't see it.

Meanwhile, Sally has flopped a pair of Aces. Her second-best card is the King from her hole cards. If someone else had also flopped a pair of Aces, but held a smaller kicker, Sally would likely be winning because of her King. You'll read more about kickers in the next chapter. In any case, Sally likes her *top pair* so much that she raises, making the bet $6.

With his powerful set, Moe could reraise, but he knows that in this structured-limit game, the bet size doubles on the next card. He decides to set a trap for Sally by just calling.

Turn

Again, stop and look at the table and work out the player's best five-card hands for yourself, now that they each have six cards to work with. Moe's hand hasn't gotten any better, but it hasn't gotten any worse: it's still quite strong. But strangely, he checks. Joe's hand *has* improved: he still has his flush draw, but the Ten on the turn gives him two pair, Jacks and Tens. He bets $6. Sally is worried that her top pair might not be the best hand anymore, but she calls anyway. The action is back to Moe, and now he springs his trap. He raises! Both Joe and Sally are forced to call his *check-raise* so they can continue.

River

What does everyone have now? Sally doesn't hold back. She bets $6. Moe raises, still confident, and Joe gives up and folds. Sally reraises and Moe realizes his hand may not be best after all and just calls.

When the smoke clears, Sally has the best possible hand with her Ace-high straight, Moe has the second-best hand with his set of Sevens, and Joe was smart to fold his third-best hand of Jacks and Tens. Sally takes down a $108 pot.

Example Two

There's no betting this time—just read the boards and the hole cards as shown in the tables, then figure out each player's best five-card poker hand and the ultimate winner.

Joe is the lowest hand, with only his pair of Aces in the hole. Sally easily beats Joe with a full house, Kings full of Tens; but Larry beats Sally just as easily with *quads*, or four-of-a-kind. Larry in turn loses to the winner, Moe, for whom the river card made a King-high straight flush.

Remember that in Hold'em, you can use one, both, or none of your hole cards in combination with the board. In this case, Moe needed only the J♠ in his hand to make the winner.

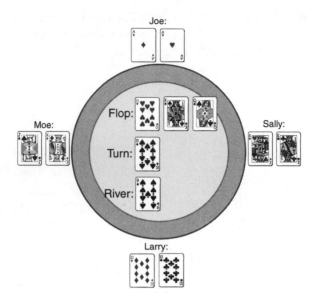

Example Two

Example Three

Here, Joe flopped top pair with his Ace, and his Queen gave him a good *kicker*, or side card. But Joe's hand never improves, and he winds up with the worst hand of the four.

Sally makes a set of Fours on the turn, but fails to improve to either a full house or quads on the river, either of which would probably have won. Her hand beats Joe's, but isn't the winner.

Moe flops a Five-high straight, and probably feels he should win, but he has the bad luck to get *counterfeited* when cards fall on the turn and the river that match his hand but don't improve it. These cards give Larry a Six-high straight using the Six in his hand, making him the winner.

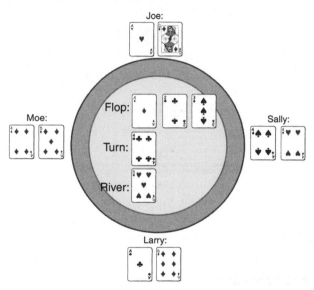

Example Three

What Next, Tex?

Judging the relative strength of your hand versus the best possible hand is an acquired skill. We recommend you get a deck of cards and start dealing five-card boards: flop, turn, and river. Skip the hole cards for now.

For each board, figure out the best possible hand, the second best, and so on. The best hand is called the *nuts*. A good Hold'em player can recognize the nuts, second nuts, and third nuts in a glance. Don't stop practicing until you can do the same. It's cheaper to learn this way than in an actual game!

The Least You Need to Know

- The dealer gives each player two hole cards; everyone then shares a three-card flop, a turn card, and a river card.

- You make your best five-card poker hand from your hole cards and the five shared cards.

- Structured-limit is the most common form of Hold'em outside of tournaments, and the easiest for beginners to learn.

- Betting moves clockwise, and always begins with the player immediately to the left of the dealer button.

What Do You Expect?

In This Chapter

- Hold'em math 101
- Simplifying things with odds and outs
- Drawing hands, made hands, and trash hands

Naturally, we're going to give you a lot of advice on how to win in the chapters to come—but there's one key idea you have to absorb first. It's not a specific strategy or secret, but an underlying method for determining the value of different plays.

Many Hold'em players have no way to look back on a hand and decide if they played it right or wrong. You will. This chapter gives you a way to evaluate strategies objectively, and adapt them to different situations.

The method goes by the somewhat scary name of *mathematical expectation*. But don't get intimidated; if you made it through sixth grade, you'll do fine. It's the concepts that are critical, not the calculating.

No Math = No Chips

Let's agree that *something* has got to guide your decision-making in poker. The question is, what? Beginning players and long-time losers often fall back on seemingly plausible strategies such as these:

- **Win as many pots as possible.** If you win most of the pots, you'll win most of the money. It stands to reason, right?

- **Play as many hands as you can.** You can't win a pot if you're not in the hand.

- **Decide which cards to play based on how they've worked out before.** You raise with pocket Aces and lose, and decide never to raise with Aces again. Or you call with 72 and flop a full house, and decide 72 is an under-appreciated gem.

Each of these approaches is incorrect and riddled with false assumptions. Following them will only cost you chips. We'll have to look elsewhere.

Expectation to the Rescue

Remember that as complicated as Hold'em can seem, there are only five things you can ever do: check, fold, call, bet, or raise. That's it. So whatever we rely on, it should apply to each of these possible choices. Just as skilled players reject the phony logic we've just examined, they also reject gut reactions like "Holy cow, I've got three-of-a-kind— I'd better raise!" Instead, what they weigh is something as hard and cold as cash itself: in each and every situation that comes up, which choice will win the most money over the long run?

That's mathematical expectation in a nutshell. But let's get just a tad more specific.

When a check, fold, call, bet, or raise loses money, we say it has *negative expectation*; when it wins money, we say it has *positive expectation*. In nearly every case, the good Hold'em player chooses the action that will maximize his positive expectation or minimize his negative expectation. For example, although a fold can never have positive expectation in the sense of winning money, it can still be your best choice if it minimizes the amount of money you lose on a particular hand.

Raise It Up

Why do we say that in "nearly every case" we want positive expectation? Why not in every case? As it happens, some clever opponents are very good at figuring out our hole cards if we always play correctly. To fool them, we can misplay a few hands—for example, raising with a hand we'd normally throw away. By sowing confusion, we hope to gain more long-term than we lose short-term. See Chapter 8 for more.

Expectation by the Numbers

It's not quite enough to describe expectation ver-
bally; as promised, we need to do a little math.

Put simply, if you stand to win D dollars if an event
occurs that has the probability P, but nothing otherwise, your expectation is D times P. Here's an
example: say you expect to win a $100 pot half the
time. Probabilities are always expressed as fractions
of 1, so we write 50 percent or ½ as .5. If we also
say that E stands for expectation, we arrive at a very
simple equation:

$$\$100 \times .5 = E$$

If we do the math, we find that your expectation in
this case is $50. End of math!

Does this mean that you'll always win $50 each
time this situation comes up? Absolutely not. You'll
win $100 about half the time, and nothing most
other times. A few hands will end in ties, and you'll
split the pot. We can't predict which times you'll
win and which times you won't—that's where luck
enters in. What we *can* say is that over the long
run, your results will come nearer and nearer to
that $50 ideal.

Raise It Up

Keep in mind that in poker, "the long run" can mean hundreds of thousands of hands. That's why players who decide which hands to play based on recent experience are making a mistake. Statistics show that pocket Aces are the best hole cards in Hold'em, but in the short-term, you can lose with them many times in a row.

Using Expectation at the Table

Okay, so you've learned this great poker concept. How do you actually make use of it? Do you sit there at the poker table like Einstein, doing math in your head?

Not the way you might think. In the heat of battle, even a professional poker player rarely resorts to the type of math we've just shown. Such equations quickly get too complicated to solve when juggling chips and cards in real-time.

And when you're first starting out, you won't be doing math at the table of *any* kind. It's just too much to handle. That's why in the chapters to come, we'll give you rules of thumb to follow, not equations.

Good players follow these rules of thumb, too. What's important to remember is that such rules are based not only on what has consistently worked well in the past, but on an understanding of mathematical expectation. Someone else has done the math so that you don't have to.

Having said all this, smart Hold'em players frequently *do* make some rough-and-ready calculations about expectation at the table. But they do so using a much more convenient style of math. Let's take a peek.

Oddly Enough

You're already familiar with odds from everyday conversation: "The odds are pretty bad." "It's a million to one against them finishing in time." "Odds are she'll get the promotion."

Odds are just a shorthand way of stating the relative chances of a favorable or unfavorable outcome for a given number of events. You get the total number of events by adding together the favorable and unfavorable outcomes.

Let's use a nonpoker example first. Say you think the odds are 2 to 1 against it raining today. What you're really saying is that for every three days like today, it won't rain on two of those days and it will rain on one of them.

Translate this to poker: you're on the river with just one opponent. The pot is $10, and now your opponent bets $10, making the total pot $20. You have to decide whether in the long run you'll make or lose money by calling that $10 bet—that is, whether calling gives you positive or negative expectation. How do you go about it?

Pot Odds

To figure out your expectation, we need to first introduce another key concept: *pot odds*. Pot odds are computed by comparing the money that has already been placed in the pot to the size of the bet to us. In this case, our pot odds are the $20 in the pot to the $10 bet, or 2 to 1.

Now here's the reason pot odds are so important: We can compare them to the odds of your winning, and presto!—we're back to knowing whether our expectation will be positive or negative. It's that simple.

Raise It Up

Pot odds exist to get compared to other odds. To make such comparison easier, it's good to get in the habit of converting denominators to 1. Say we're contemplating a $70 pot and a $30 bet: instead of leaving our pot odds as 7 to 3, we can guesstimate them as just under 2.5 to 1. (The exact answer is 2⅓ to 1, but you'll rarely require such precision.)

In this case, let's say we think our chances of winning that $20 pot are 3 to 1 against. So once out of every four times we'll win $20, and the other three times we'll lose $10, for a combined loss of $30. That means a $10 loss overall. On average, we're losing $2.50 each time—definitely a negative expectation.

On the other hand, if our chances of winning are 2 to 1 against, we'll make $20 once out of every three times and lose $10 twice, breaking exactly even. We can call or not call as we choose and it won't make any difference in the long run.

And if our chances of winning are better than 2 to 1—say, dead even at 1 to 1— we've got a guaranteed long-term winner on our hands. For every two tries, we'll win that $20 pot once and lose our $10 bet once, giving us a positive expectation of $10 each time we call.

Outs and Odds

But just how do we go about calculating our chances of winning in the first place? If we don't have that number, we won't have anything to compare against our pot odds.

In some cases, math isn't the most important factor in assessing where you stand. When you're head-to-head with a single foe, the winning hand could be a monster or a mouse (though mice are far more common). In such cases, psychology, intuition, and logic help more than math in gauging your chances.

But it's different when you're drawing to a hand such as a straight, flush, or a full house, especially against many opponents. Such hands are usually powerful enough to give us confidence that if we catch the right cards on the turn or river, we'll win; if not, we'll probably lose. So all we need is a way to figure the odds of making our draw.

Here's a common example. Let's say your hole cards are the Ace and Eight of Hearts. The flop and turn put two Hearts on board, so if the river is a Heart, you'll make an Ace-high flush. Let's further say that you're confident a flush of any sort will win, let alone an Ace-high. So what are your chances?

It's surprisingly easy to calculate. You've seen six cards—your two hole cards and the four cards making up the flop and turn. That leaves 46 unseen cards in the deck. You've also seen four Hearts—the two on board and the two in your hand. That leaves nine Hearts left out of the 13 in the deck; these potentially winning cards are your *outs*.

Assuming you'll lose if you *don't* make the flush, your chances of winning now become 37 to 9, or 5.1 against. You can now compare this to your pot odds: let's say the pot contains $40 and the bet to you is $10—if you don't figure to make any more money on the river, you should fold, since your 5-to-1 odds of making the flush are worse than your 4-to-1 pot odds.

Talk Like a Texan

Outs in Hold'em are the number of cards that you think will make you a winning hand. **Tainted outs** are as insidious as they sound—cards that give you a good hand, but make your opponent a better hand: a heart that gives you a flush might make someone else a full house, for example. It's easy to count your outs, but knowing if they're tainted calls for considerable skill.

But let's say you think you'll be able to win two extra $10 bets on the river should you make your flush. You can mentally add that additional $20 to the existing $40 pot, giving you 6-to-1 pot odds. Now your pot odds are better than your drawing odds, so a call here gives you positive expectation—even though many times you'll miss your flush and have to fold the river.

Implied Odds

This notion of counting on future bets if you get lucky and make a big drawing hand is called *implied odds*. While pot odds exist only in relation to the current pot, implied odds exist only with more cards and bets to come.

Just as for flushes, outs and odds can be calculated for drawing to such hands as straights, three-of-a-kinds, full houses, and so on. In each case, the comparison is between the cards left in the deck that won't help you versus those that will.

As we said, you won't be working with odds and outs quite yet—the rules of thumb you'll learn will be enough. Just for fun, though, flip to Appendix B and take a look at the odds tables there. Good players are so motivated, they learn these by heart—something to bear in mind if you get serious.

Drawing Hands, Made Hands, and Trash Hands

You may have noticed the term *drawing hand* being thrown about in the preceding section. As we said, the archetypal drawing hands are straights and flushes: unless you actually make your straight or flush, you generally fold on the river, since you can't even beat a lowly pair of Deuces.

The opposite of a drawing hand is a *made hand*—a hand that doesn't need to improve to have a chance of being the winner. A pair of Kings in the hole is a good example, since Kings will win many a pot unimproved.

It's true that pocket Kings *can* improve, but this doesn't happen very often. In the outs tables in Appendix B, you'll see that while a flush draw has nine outs and a straight draw has eight outs, two Kings in the hole usually have only their two fellow regents as outs if they hope to improve to three-of-a-kind.

Aside from pocket pairs, another common made hand is top pair. Typically you make this hand when you hold two big cards, for example AQ, and the flop pairs one of them—in this case, coming either Ace-high or Queen-high. Naturally, the bigger your top pair, the better.

What Drawing Hands Want

Lots of other players in the pot, and a cheap initial price. This will give you good pot odds to see the flop and good implied odds if you do flop a draw. After all, most of the time you won't flop even the ghost of a draw, and will have to fold then and there. More on this in the next chapter.

What Made Hands Want

Preferably to be up against a couple of other weaker made hands or worse. For example, if you flopped a pair of Jacks, you'd be happy to have a player who flopped a pair of Nines as your sole opponent—neither hand has much chance of improving, and unless the Nines improve, they'll never beat the Jacks.

What made hands *don't* want is to be surrounded by a lot of drawing hands on a flop that favors the drawing hands. This is one reason why players with two big cards usually raise preflop—to cut down the number of draws. Otherwise it's like a bear surrounded by a pack of wolves: the bear may be bigger, but the numbers favor the wolves.

Raise It Up

The biggest exception to made hands not liking company is the single best hand there is—pocket Aces. One of the reasons pocket rockets are the best hand is that they win the most money no matter how many players are in the pot. Mingling with the mob or tête-à-tête—Aces are happy either way.

For example, let's say a player raises before the flop with AQ but gets a host of callers. The flop comes with a Queen, giving our hero a pair of Queens. If this player is unlucky enough to be up against a middle straight draw, a smaller pocket pair, and a flush draw, as many as 17 unseen cards in the deck could give someone a better hand than Queens.

This may not sound too bad—except that if everyone sticks around for both the turn and the river, the probability that someone will beat the Queens is roughly 60 percent! This nasty situation (from the made hand's point of view) is called *reverse implied odds.* Keep it in mind as we go forward.

What Trash Hands Want

To be thrown into the muck each time they're dealt to you.

Trash hands are hole cards like 83, J2, and so on. They can't flop a draw, have little chance of flopping a winning top pair, and you will be dealt them more than any other kind of hand. The only rational response is to fold them, but do you know why?

It's not because they're ugly—it's because they have negative expectation. Do the math, and you find they don't make the winning hand often enough to justify paying even a fraction of a bet for them. Ever.

Many losing players love *suited trash*—hands where both hole cards are suited, but far apart in rank, such as J2s or 83s. These players reason that such hands have just as good a chance of flopping a flush draw as suited hands where the cards are close in rank, such as JTs or T8s. The problem is that the *only* way suited trash can win is with a flush, whereas a hand like JTs can also make a straight or in rare cases top pair that holds up.

These extra ways to win give hands like JTs positive expectation when played right, whereas suited trash has negative expectation unless you're in the blinds and can get in cheap. Players who don't know about expectation will keep paying for suited trash over and over, remembering the few big pots they win and forgetting all the chips they dribble away in between.

Delusions of Squander

For fun, let's revisit the list of losing notions we started out with and pinpoint the exact problem with each. Try covering up the answers and thinking first to see how much you've learned.

Q: Winning most of the pots means winning most of the money, right?

A: This would be true if all pots were the same size, but they're not. A better strategy is to try and make the few pots you're likely to win as big as possible. This is one of the reasons you raise with big pocket pairs like AA and KK before the flop: you have a far better chance of winning than usual, so you're seeking the maximum donation from everyone at the table.

Q: If I play as many hands as possible, doesn't that give me more chances to win?

A: Hold'em isn't a lottery, where every ticket has the same chance of winning; good cards have positive expectation, and bad cards have negative expectation. If you're getting dealt nothing but bad cards, keep folding until your luck changes.

Q: If you see it with your own eyes, it must be true, so what better guide than personal experience to rate your hole cards?

A: That kind of thinking is so short-term you're liable to catch amnesia. Remember, you're in quest of an ideal. You want to play the cards that average a profit over time, not the cards that got lucky yesterday.

The Least You Need to Know

- Mathematical expectation—whether you'll make or lose money in the long run—is the secret behind every decision to check, fold, call, bet, or raise.

- Keep track of your pot odds by comparing the pot size to the size of the current bet; compare this ratio to your chances of winning to determine your best play.

- Experienced players calculate their chances of making a winning flush or straight by counting the cards in the deck that will help them, but beginners can rely on rules of thumb.

- Drawing hands, such as straights and flushes, want lots of company and no raises before the flop to ensure positive expectation.

- Trash hands are your most common hole cards, but they have such negative expectation that you should nearly always refuse to play them—even if they're suited.

Getting the Right Price Preflop

In This Chapter

- Luck before the flop versus luck after
- Why position matters
- Hold'em hand groups
- Picking good hands by position
- Preflop quiz

It's often been said that the most important decision you make in Hold'em is what hole cards to play, and what to throw away. And we don't disagree. The easiest way to be a consistent loser in Hold'em is to play too many hands before the flop.

The good news is that preflop hand selection is also the easiest part of the game to learn. Let's take a look at the hands you will and won't be playing, and why.

Abbreviations for Hole Cards

By their very nature, abbreviations for hole cards help classify preflop hands into one type or another. This will give you a jump on learning good preflop play, which is all about creating the right circumstances for a given type of hand.

Hole Card Abbreviations

Example	Meaning
AKs, JTs, 98s	The "s" indicates the cards are suited—for example, the Ace and King of Clubs and the Ace and King of Hearts are both written AKs.
AK, T8, 98	Without an "s," these same cards are offsuit; that is, not suited.
Ax, Kx, Qx	The "x" after a face card refers to any card below a Nine. Here, Kx could mean anything from K8 to K2.
Axs, Kxs, Qxs	The same type of hand as above, only suited.

Maneuvering Before the Flop

Hold'em is really two different games: before the flop, and after. The addition of three flop cards all at once has a galvanic effect on the value of your hand. Sometimes it becomes super-charged; more often it gets toasted.

Say you're dealt a powerhouse like AKs, or "Big Slick." You raise and get called by a loosey-goosey player holding J8, a hand whose long-term value is roughly that of snail slime. Lo, the flop comes JJ8, giving snail slime a full house and Big Slick a fast trip to the muck pile.

But don't get the idea that the flop is all that matters, and start playing every hand, waiting until after the flop to decide whether to fold. Hands like AKs flop good far more often than hands like J8— and when AKs and J8 both flop good, AKs will almost always come out on top. You've got to think selectively, or your chips will disappear so fast you'll think someone bored a hole in the table.

Given the uncertainty of the flop and the importance of being frugal, your goal before the flop should be to provide your hand with the circumstances in which it does best. If you think you can't arrange those circumstances, it's often best to fold.

For example, high-card hands that hope to flop top pair should usually raise before the flop to knock out draws. Taking this logic a step further, if enough players are already in that a raise won't narrow the field, you're actually better off folding some of the weaker high-card hands.

Raise It Up _____

Don't count on getting good hands often. There are 169 possible two-card starting hands you can be dealt in Hold'em—and more than half of them are so weak you should almost never play them. Two unpaired low cards of different suits are among the worst hands. The very best hands feature two high cards, with a pair of Aces the leader of the pack.

The Imposition of Position

Another factor is your position relative to the dealer button. It's so vital that special terms have evolved to describe it. Here we're talking about a full 10-player game:

- **Under the gun** means the player first to act before the flop. That's the person to the immediate left of the big blind. As the term suggests, he's under considerable pressure.

- **Early position** before the flop refers to the under-the-gun player plus the two players to his left; after the flop, it includes the blinds, since they will now be acting before anyone else if they're still in.

- **Middle position** refers to the next three or four players.

- **Late position** includes the *cutoff*, the player immediately before the button, as well as the button himself.

Talk Like a Texan

The **cutoff** is so named because the player in this seat can try to "cut off" the player on the button by raising before the flop. If the button folds to this ploy, the cutoff inherits his privilege of being last to act on every street after the flop.

Position affects how much information you have, and that affects your ability to safely play certain kinds of hands. For example, in early position, you don't know how many players or raises will come after you, so you've got to be cautious and play only big hands—especially when you're new to the game.

For example, if you're dealt a potential drawing hand like JTs, you've usually got to muck it, for fear of a raise behind you or of getting too few callers.

In late position, you know more and have less to fear. If a lot of players have called with no raise, those JTs become eminently playable. And if everyone has folded to you, you can raise with Swiss cheese in an attempt to steal the blinds.

Hold'em Hand Groups

We've arrived at the juicy section of this chapter: the classification of playable hands into different groups.

These hand groups are something of an illusion, like dividing a piano keyboard into octaves: in reality the keyboard is a continuous sequence of notes from top to bottom, but the concept of octaves lets us talk about groups of notes near each other.

Likewise, Hold'em hands are fluid by nature, slipping up and down in value according to the situation. Experience will eventually teach you to judge each hand on its own merits, but the hand groups are a useful crutch when starting out.

Take a moment to scan the chart, then refer back to it as necessary as each group is discussed.

Hold'em Hand Groups

Offsuit Raisers	Suited Raisers	
AK, AQ	AKs, AQs	
KQ, AJ	KQs, AJs	
AT, KJ	ATs, KJs	
A9, KT, QJ	A9s, KTs, QJs	
Ax, Kx, JT	Ax, Kxs, JTs	
Big Pairs	**Medium Pairs**	**Baby Pairs**
AA, KK, QQ	TT, 99	66, 22
JJ	88, 77	

Straight-Flush Draws	Straight-Only Draws	Gapped Straight-Flush Draws
JTs, T9s	JT	Ts, J9s
87s, 76s	T9, 98, 76	T8s, 97s

Notes on the Hand Groups

If you don't see a hand listed in the previous table, chances are it's rarely playable unless you're in the blinds and can see the flop for free or for a fraction of a bet.

Within each group, hands are listed in order of strength. For example, you can play the top Offsuit Raiser, AK, in any position. But the hands on the last rung in this group—Ax, Kx, and JT—are almost unplayable as raising hands unless you're the small blind trying to steal from the big blind. This is largely due to fear of *domination*.

Other hand groups are less variable: for example, hands belonging to the Baby Pairs and the various Draws can be played similarly, despite differences in relative strength. Exploring such differences can wait until you gain experience.

Talk Like a Texan

Domination occurs when a raiser's hand is so much better than your hand that you almost can't beat him—even though yours is a raising hand, too. An example is AK versus AQ. If an Ace comes on the flop, the AQ will find it hard to fold, even though it's doomed by its second-best kicker. And even a powerful hand like pocket Kings can be dominated if it's up against pocket Aces—a smaller pair is about a 4 to 1 underdog head-up against a bigger pair. To avoid domination, it's generally best not to call raises unless you hold a hand near the top end of the raiser's likely range of hands given his position.

Playable Hands by Position

Position is the single most critical factor before the flop. So the easiest way to start learning the hand groups is by changing seats around the table, seeing in each case what we can play.

As before, we'll assume a full table with 10 players. Often that won't be the case, but adjusting for fewer players is easy. Say for example that there are only seven players. The under-the-gun player is now in the same exact seat as the middle-position player would be if the game were full—so he should play his hands the same way as if he were in middle position in a full game, and everyone ahead of him had folded.

Or say there are just five players. In that case, the player under the gun is in the same seat as the cutoff in a full game. He should play his hands exactly as if he *were* the cutoff in a full game and, once again, everyone ahead of him had folded.

Early Position: Tight Is Right

As we've stated, if you're in the first few seats before the flop, you lack the information to safely play anything but your very best hands. At all but the most *passive* tables, you're forced to fold drawing hands for fear of a raise behind you. Likewise you play only your top raising hands, for fear of domination.

Talk Like a Texan

> **Passive** is at the opposite end of **aggressive** in poker. Passive players rarely raise before the flop without an absolute monster, while aggressive players raise whenever a good opportunity comes along. You'll learn more about this and other ways of categorizing your opponents in the chapters to come.

Early, and No One Has Raised

Go ahead and raise with all your big pairs, and in a *tight* game—a game where few players tend to call before the flop—raise as well with the two biggest medium pairs, TT and 99. With QQ, KK, and AA you don't care how many people call, but with 99, TT, and even JJ, you're hoping to get just one or two callers to boost the chances your pair will be the best hand on the flop.

Also raise with the top rungs in the Offsuit Raisers and Suited Raisers—AK, AQ, AKs, and AQs. If you're adventurous, you can raise with KQs and AJs as well, but be aware that these latter hands are more easily dominated. The only reason you can raise with them is because they're suited, giving you an extra way to win.

Raise It Up

Here's a trick often used by experienced players: once in a while, limp AA and KK instead of raising—that is, just call with them, as if you have an ordinary or even a weak hand. What you're hoping for is that you'll get some limpers and then a raise, allowing you to put in a second raise. The pot will be huge by the time you get to the flop, and you'll have an enormous head start.

Fold all other hands in this position for now. Certain types of games let you play drawing hands up front, but you can only judge this after you've gained considerable experience.

Early, and Someone Has Raised

If the under-the-gun player raises and you're next in line, you must now truly play tight: until evidence shows otherwise, assume the raiser has at least as good a hand as you'd have in his spot. If no one else calls, you'll be head-up with the raiser, so whatever you're holding had better be good.

With QQ, KK, AA, and possibly JJ, your best play is not to call but to reraise. These hands are good enough that there's a chance you're better than the raiser if he's holding a smaller pair or a hand like AQ or AK. With AKs you can call or reraise, depending on whether you want to lure other players in so you'll win a big pot should you make a flush. For similar reasons, you can chance calling with AQs—but only if the table is playing loose enough that you'll get company.

Middle Position: A Little Looser

Sitting in the middle of the lineup, the possibilities expand, and your hand selection can expand a little more, too.

Middle, and No One Has Opened

When you *open the pot*, you become the first player to voluntarily put chips into the pot, by either calling or raising the big blind. So either you're first to act, or else everyone before you has folded.

When opening in middle position, it's usually best to raise, for the same reasons as you would under the gun. But now you can raise with hands as weak as KQ and AJ, as well as those already mentioned. And you're definitely raising with TT and 99.

Middle, and Several Players Have Called

The presence of two to four callers in the pot ahead of you means you must tighten up a little with raises, but can loosen up with your better drawing hands.

You can still raise with your powerhouses: AK, AQ, AKs, AQs, all the big pairs, and even KQs and AJs. But you need to think about whether to raise with a hand slightly weaker than these such as KQ and AJ. Many good players do, but only if they feel they're up against weak opposition. When you're just starting out, it's fine to call with hands such as these and hope for a good flop.

You can limp drawing hands on the order of JTs, T9s, 88, 77, and in a passive game: QTs and J9s. You're hoping no one will raise behind you.

Middle, and There's a Raise with No Callers Yet

This depends on where the raise came from. If it's from under the gun, you must still fold all but your very best hands.

But if the raise comes from the middle player just in front of you, you can call or possibly reraise with even the weakest of your early-position raising hands. The raiser could still have a powerhouse, but given his position, it's less likely. For example, you'd probably reraise with AQ.

Middle, and There's a Raise with Several Callers

You can play all the quality hands we mentioned before, but now you can consider cautiously adding JTs, TT, and 99. But you must be careful: if you don't get a great flop, you'll have to fold. If you do hit a great flop, you stand to win a bigger pot than usual.

With JTs, you're hoping for a straight or flush draw; with TT and 99, you're looking to flop either a set or top pair. Top pair isn't very likely, and neither is a set, but the two possibilities combined are just enough.

Late Position: Time to Limp or Else Get Aggressive

By now you have lots of information and much less concern about what someone will do in back of you—only the blinds remain. But you still must play the right hands for the situation.

Late, and No One Has Opened

Here's where the weaker members of the Offsuit and Suited Raisers come into their own. As cutoff or even a seat before, you can open-raise with AT and KJ, plus their suited variants. As dealer, you can open-raise with A9, KT, and QJs.

With so few players left, there's a good chance your relatively weak raising hand is in fact the best hand. Your goal here is to steal the blinds or get head-up with one other weaker hand—but be aware that if you're playing in a casino at a very low-limit table, the rake may be so brutal that a purely steal hand should be folded. See Chapter 8 for exactly why.

Late, and Many Players Have Called

If lots of players are in and no one has raised, you'll be able to limp your full range of drawing hands, including all the Straight-Flush Draws and Gapped Straight-Flush Draws. Most of the time, you'll have to fold when the flop misses your hand. But when you *do* hit, having this many players in means you'll have a shot at winning an extra-large pot.

Late, and There's a Raise with No Callers Yet

Position counts here. If the raise came from an early position, you must play tight as before. But if, for example, the cutoff raises, you can chance a reraise with as little as AT, A9s, or 66. Your goal is to get head-up and hope he was trying to steal.

If you've got a monster like AA, you might want to just call a late raise to disguise the nature of your hand, but this is a riskier option, one you'll have to gain experience with.

Late, and There's a Raise with Many Callers

This isn't too dissimilar from a middle raise with several callers: JTs and the medium pairs are playable with five or more players in the pot ahead of you. And if it's a *family pot*, with the whole table calling so far, you can call with the baby pairs and the smaller Straight-Flush draws. The pot will be so big that the extra price you're paying to draw is worth it.

The only thing to be careful about is a game where players love to gamble and raising is epidemic: it's one thing to pay two bets for the privilege of drawing with a hand like 87s, but if the action moves back around and an early limper puts in a reraise just for fun, it hurts your expectation. Therefore, consider the likelihood of a reraise before calling with your weaker hands.

The Blinds: Free Looks and Bargains

When you're in the small blind, you'll already have part of a bet in the pot. In the big blind, you'll have a whole bet invested. This causes many players to automatically complete the bet in the small blind or call raises in the big blind. But you shouldn't do anything automatically. Instead, consider the following strategies for different situations.

Watch Your Chips

Beware of calling too many raises when you're in the blinds, especially the small blind. Sure, you're getting a discount, but that doesn't mean that paying a bet and a half or a bet and two thirds for total trash suddenly becomes a great deal. If you were in the market for a good used car, would you buy a wreck with no tires or motor, just because it was cheap?

In the Blinds, and No Raise

In the small blind, go ahead and call with any hand in any of the hand groups. With many players in, you can even call with suited trash, a hand you'd normally fold. The discount you're getting plus your good pot odds have made the difference.

In either the small or big blind, with hands as good as KK, AA, AQs, AKs, and AK, you should prefer to raise to build the pot. You're so much better than the average starting hand that you want more money in for those times you flop a monster. If only a few players are in, you can also raise with QQ. If it's just the dealer limping in, go ahead and raise with any of the hands you'd raise with in early position.

In the Blinds, and a Raise

If four or more players have already called the raise, or look like they'll call when the action gets back to them, you can call in the small blind with your better drawing hands and the hands you'd raise with in early position. And you should put in a second raise yourself with KK, AA, AKs, and AQs. The big blind can raise with these hands as well, and can also call with any drawing hand, not just the better draws.

If no one has called the raiser yet, or if there's just one or two callers, you must tighten up consider-ably. JTs might be the weakest of the drawing hands you'd call with in the small blind.

Again, consider the raiser's position: if he raised under the gun and you're contemplating being the sole caller in either of the blinds, you'll need a powerful hand. The big blind can play a trifle looser than the small blind, but stay away from dominated hands.

For example, if the raise is from under the gun and you're in the big blind with AT, you're better off folding even though your hand is fairly respectable. There's too much chance you'll flop an Ace, call all the way, and get shown AQ, AK, or AJs. You'd ac-tually be better off calling with a hand like 98s or 88 that seeks to exploit flops with small cards.

Quiz on Preflop Play

Let's see how much you've learned. Again, we'll assume a full game with all 10 seats filled.

Q: The under-the-gun player limps in, and you're next. What do you do with AJ? 76s? TT?

A: *AJ:* Raise if you think it will narrow the field, but be wary if you get reraised. A better play might be to fold and wait for a slightly higher-quality hand in this spot, such as AQ. *76s:* Fold. You don't know whether enough players will come in without a raise behind you, and if you flop a draw, you'll be out of position for the entire hand. *TT:* Raise. It'll give you more ways to win. If you get lots of callers and flop a set, you could win a huge pot. On the other hand, if you get just one or two callers, your Tens now stand a better chance of winning even if you *don't* flop a set.

Q: Everyone folds to a middle position player who open-raises. He gets one caller before the action comes to you on the button. What do you do with JJ? 76s? AQ?

A: *JJ:* Reraise. You've probably got the best hand and you want to make them pay to see a flop. If your raise knocks out the blinds, that's good, too; your big pair will play much better, with less fear of overcards, if you can narrow the field. *76s:* Fold. This smallish drawing hand requires a family pot or position in the blinds before it can call a raise. *AQ:* It's a toss-up between calling and raising. Like

JJ, this hand would do better if you could narrow the field, but unlike JJ, you don't have a made hand yet. If the raiser is a tough player, calling is best.

Q: You're in the small blind, with four limpers to you and no raise yet. Just half a bet, and you're in—but of course you can raise, too. What do you do with 44? QQ? 96?

A: *44:* Call. This is a good drawing hand with many callers and the discount. *QQ:* Raise. You've probably got the best hand here, so go ahead and raise. Sure, someone may hit an Ace or King on the flop, but for now you want to make them pay for the privilege. And against typical limping hands, like 9Ts or 33, you have a crushing advantage. *96:* Fold. Yes, you're getting a discount and your pot odds look good—but your expectation is still negative.

The Least You Need to Know

- Be selective in choosing which hole cards to play, based on your position relative to the dealer, whether anyone has raised yet, and how many players have already called.

- The earlier your position, the less you know and the more you have to fear, so the stronger your hands must be.

- The later your position, the more you know and the less you have to fear, allowing you to play more draws and raise with weaker hands.

- Hand groups are a convenient way to remember the value of different hole cards, as well as the conditions they favor.

- The blinds give you a discount, allowing you to play more hands—but you've still got to be selective.

Garbage to Gold (and Vice Versa)

In This Chapter

- Fitting the flop
- Tough choices on the turn
- Maximizing the river
- Postflop quiz

So you did your best to pick good starting cards—but now the *flop* has come, and you and your opponents are staring at three new cards face-up in the middle of the table. Depending on the nature of your hole cards, these three new cards may make you want to jump out of your chair—or slide under it.

No matter how strong your hole cards—even those mythic pocket Aces—you'll usually be looking for help on the flop. Of course, so will your opponents. The challenge now becomes calculating not just the objective value of your hand by itself, but how it stacks up against the possible hands your opponents may hold.

And there's still the *turn* and *river* to come! With each fresh community card, you must assess and reassess. Do I have the best hand now? Am I drawing to make the best hand? Which cards can help me? Which cards can hurt me? And what are the other players holding, given the *board* and the betting?

It's a tall order. But in this chapter, you learn how to size up these dicey situations and choose your best play.

 Talk Like a Texan

> Remember, the **board** refers to the five common cards shared by all the players. The **flop** refers to the first three board cards. The **turn** is the fourth card. And the **river** is the fifth card. It completes the board and gives all players seven cards to work with in making their best poker hand.

Be Flexible on the Flop

The first rule is to forget about how pretty or ugly your hole cards looked preflop. Whether you were jamming with pocket Kings or limping a dog of a drawing hand, it's chips under the bridge. How your cards mesh or don't mesh with the flop is all that matters now.

With five cards on the board and only two more to go, you're seeing 71 percent of the cards you'll ever see. This is your chance to re-evaluate the present and future value of your hand.

At the same time, you also have to factor in the betting, your position at the table, the size of the pot, and the odds your hand will improve by catching a helping card on the turn.

Raise It Up _____

A weak hand in a big pot can be worth more than a strong hand in a small one. For example, let's say you have a 20 percent chance (1 in 5) of winning a $100 pot. In that situation, your hand is "worth" $20. Now what if you have a better hand—say one with a 50 percent chance of winning—but the pot is just $30? This hand is worth just $15.

This method of valuing a hand is known as pot equity. In small pots, you may find your pot equity won't justify calling even a single bet, while in big pots even a relatively slim chance of winning can make it well worth your while to play on.

In calculating this last factor, there's an added consideration: might a card that helps you help an opponent even more? For example, if you hold 89 and the flop comes TJ3, a Queen on the turn can make you a straight, but it would also make a higher straight for anyone holding K9 or AK.

To help you get a feel for playing the flop, the next few pages analyze some common situations. Also included is a table, "Matching Your Hole Cards to the Flop," that lays out some specific situations.

Made Hands on the Flop

Sometimes you'll have a hand that's likely to be the best on the flop. Say you started with KQ and the flop comes QT7. You've "flopped good," making top pair (Queens) with the second highest possible kicker (the King).

You'll usually want to play this hand aggressively, by putting in a bet or raise. There's a good chance you're winning, so you want to get as many bets here as you can from the other players.

Furthermore, with this flop, someone could be drawing to a straight with a hand like 89, to a Q with a worse kicker or even a hand like T9, middle pair plus a straight draw. Most of the time they'll miss their draw on the turn and river, and in the meantime you certainly don't want to let them draw for free when they could be paying you for the privilege.

Drawing Hands on the Flop

Other times you'll be the one drawing. For example, if you limped in with A♥6♥ and the flop came K♥9♥2♠, you'd have a draw to the best possible flush.

You'll frequently want to play a drawing hand more passively than a made hand. In this example, anyone with a pair is ahead of you right now, and it's about 2 to 1 against you actually making a flush by the river. So if there's a bet to you, you should often just call. If you raise, you'll not only be putting money in with a hand that's currently losing, but you may also cause other players in the hand to fold. You don't really want that to happen—you want them around on the turn or river to call your bets if you *do* make your flush.

Sometimes, though, you *will* want to bet or raise with a draw. Remember, we just said the odds of making your flush by the river are about 2 to 1 against. That means you're actually getting pot odds here if two or more opponents call your extra action. What's more, a bet or raise on the flop might make opponents check to you on the turn. Then if the turn card doesn't make your flush, you can check along and see the river card for free. Another reason to get aggressive in this example is the Ace you hold as part of your hand. By raising on the flop, you may chase out a player who also holds an Ace, but with a better kicker. Should an Ace come on the turn or river, your now uncontested pair of Aces may well prove the winner.

Matching Your Hole Cards to the Flop

Hole Cards	Flop
AA	K82 of different suits

What you like: This is a very good flop for you. Your top pair is likely to be the best hand and there are no flush or straight possibilities.

What to watch for: All you really have to fear is someone with pocket Kings, Eights, or Deuces who would now have three-of-a-kind, or maybe a hand like K8s that has flopped two pair. Bet if checked to and raise if someone else bets.

55	5AQ with two cards of the same suit

What you like: You've got a strong and well-concealed *set* of Fives. Anyone with an Ace or Queen is likely to give you action.

What to watch for: If someone calls all bets on this two-suited flop, or even tosses in a raise, they could have a flush draw. If a third suited card hits on the turn, and that player starts betting or raising, he may have made his flush. The good news is that if the board pairs on the river, you'll make a full house and beat him.

AKs	678 all one suit, different from yours

What you like: Not much. Your powerful starting hand has completely missed this flop. If you have only one or two opponents, you may have the best hand—for now.

What to watch for: It's relatively unlikely, but you could already be losing badly to a made flush or straight, or even a set or two pair. Pairing an Ace or King on the turn won't be enough to beat these hands. If there's a bet and a raise in front of you, it could be folding time.

Hole Cards	Flop
JTs	6QK with one card of your suit

What you like: You have an *open-ended draw* (meaning that you can make a straight with either a Nine or an Ace) to the best possible straight, plus a *backdoor* flush draw if the turn and river cards are both your suit.

What to watch for: Anyone with a King or Queen is beating you right now. You have eight outs (four Nines and four Aces) to give you the highest possible straight, so you won't fold. But for now you'll usually want to be a caller, not a bettor. And remember that hitting a Jack or Ten on the turn or river is unlikely to win for you—not only would a King or Queen still beat you, but the board could now give somebody else a straight.

Position on the Flop and Beyond

Your position relative to the other players is at least as important on the flop, turn, and river as it was preflop. Whenever you're the first to bet or check, everyone else has an advantage over you. They can fold their weak hands, or bet or raise with their strong ones. Plus if you check, they can use their position to bet a weak hand, in hopes you'll fold.

When you're last to act, *you* have the same advantage. You no longer have to guess what the other players might do, and this lets you play more aggressively. For example, say you limped in behind four other players with A5s on the button. If the flop comes A93 of different suits and everyone checks, you can bet with a fair amount of confidence that your pair of Aces is best, despite your rag kicker.

One way to turn all this around and make early position an advantage with certain hands is by using the *check-raise*. Say you've flopped a moderately good hand such as top pair. You'd like to protect it by betting enough to make opponents either fold or pay too much to draw. But you're in early position—if you bet here, you could easily get several callers. What to do?

Try this: check meekly, as if the flop missed you. Hopefully everyone else will check to a late-position player. If he bets, you'll now have the chance to raise and confront the other players with the prospect of calling not just one bet, but two.

Of course if everyone checks, you can't raise. So it's best to use this maneuver when you think someone *will* bet. Also, the exact effect depends on the position of the bettor. For example, let's say you're first to act and there are four players behind you. If you check and the next player bets, the other players will have already folded or else called the single bet before the action gets back to you. In that situation, a check-raise isn't likely to knock anyone out.

Raise It Up _____

Back in Chapter 2, we emphasized the need to always know the nuts—that is, the best hand that someone can hold with whatever common cards are showing. Just remember that most times, no one will actually *have* the nuts. If you've got a hand like a pair of Nines and the flop comes AA7, often no one has an Ace. There are only two Aces left in the deck, so you very well may have the best hand—even though the board looks terrifying.

To the Turn

With a fourth card on the board, your hand has either improved or it hasn't. If it hasn't, there's now only one more chance for help instead of two.

Another crucial factor is that in most limit games, the bet size doubles on the turn. For example, in a $2/$4 game, the maximum bet is $2 before the flop and on the flop, but $4 on the turn and river.

This means that while the flop may be easy street, the turn is the tough side of town. Many low-limit players will call the flop with almost anything, but a call on the turn often betrays either a real hand or a solid draw.

Moreover, the increased bet size induces seemingly paradoxical behavior on the part of players who flop extremely powerful hands such as *trips*, sets, straights, or flushes. You might expect them to play the flop aggressively, but in fact many prefer to check and call as meekly as your Aunt Edna.

> **Talk Like a Texan**
>
> From Chapter 2, you'll remember that a set is three-of-a-kind made by holding a pocket pair when a third card of that rank is on the board. You can also make three-of-a-kind by matching one of your hole cards with two paired cards on the board. That hand is called **trips**.

Why? First, a player with a monster doesn't want to drive off her customers—she'd rather have as many players as possible stick around. Second, by just calling any flop bets, she hopes to lull the bettor into betting the turn as well. Now when she raises, she'll earn twice as much with the double-size bet.

Whether you're looking at the nuts or nada, the turn calls for some planning on your part. With only one card to go, you now have to consider not just how to play your hand here, but how to play the river as well. Let's look at some typical scenarios.

Made Hands on the Turn

If you think you're ahead, you'll want to get your money in now to charge stubborn callers. Besides, often the pot has gotten big enough that you won't mind if everyone folds to your turn bet and you take down the money right here.

Sometimes the turn will complete a draw for you. Typically you'll have the nuts on the turn, with a strong likelihood that they'll hold up—for example, an Ace-high flush on an unpaired board. In the best case, you'll hold not just the nuts, but the pure nuts: no matter what card comes on the river, it can't make a hand that will beat yours. An example of this would be when you've flopped a four flush with 10♥9♥ on a board like Q♥8♥4♣ and the turn makes you a straight flush with the J♥. Your only problem is figuring out how to milk the maximum number of bets from the other players!

Unfortunately, most hands aren't this strong. Often you'll have a good hand, such as top pair, that may still be the best on the turn, but continues to be pursued by several opponents. They're hoping for a good river card, but most of the time they won't get it.

Bet or raise strongly to lower their odds and charge them the maximum for their draw, just as you would on the flop. In any one hand, they may draw out on you, but you can't let this make you forego betting when you have a substantial advantage on every extra bet that goes in. Sometimes the turn card makes a straight or flush possible right then and there. If a normally passive opponent starts raising the moon at this point and you hold only a fair hand such as top pair, you'll probably want to fold—you can't possibly improve to beat the hand they're representing. But if the raiser is tricky or aggressive, you may be better off calling, especially if the pot is large. Likewise, if you hold a set, you have a *redraw*, meaning your hand can still improve on the river to beat a straight or flush. In that case, a call is again in order.

Drawing Hands on the Turn

Because of the sudden jump on the turn to a double-size bet, you must be extra-careful of your drawing odds versus your pot odds. For example, you might be able to call a single bet and still have positive expectation, but not a bet and a raise. Smart opponents who've put you on a draw will often raise the turn solely for the purpose of hurting your odds or knocking you out, whether or not their own hand is strong.

In calculating your odds, think carefully about how many outs you *really* have to improve to a winning hand. It can be quite expensive when your hand improves on the river, but not enough to win.

For example, say you're holding A♠K♠ and the board on the turn is J♠8♠3♥9♦. It's tempting to think that in addition to your nine flush outs, you've got an extra four outs by counting the remaining Aces and Kings not of your suit. But would making top pair on the river be enough to win? If you have only one opponent, there's a good chance it would.

However, let's say it's a four-way pot and the cutoff's eyes lit up at the sight of the Nine. If he now starts raising like he's turned the straight, you'll probably have to beat that hand to win. That puts you back at your nine flush outs, not the 13 combined outs you were hoping for.

Betting the Turn

It can be correct to bet the turn even when you don't have a made hand or a draw, especially when you have one opponent who may also be weak.

Let's say you raised preflop with AK and got two callers. The flop came T73 of different suits, you bet out again, and one player folded. Now the turn brings a Four. If your sole remaining opponent has so much as a pair of Deuces, he's ahead. Nevertheless, it's often correct to bet your hand again.

Why? First, the larger bet size and your persistent aggression may convince your opponent to fold a better hand than yours, such as the Deuces we just mentioned. Second, if he's on a draw, your Ace-high may beat him if he doesn't make that draw. By betting, you're making him call a bet at even odds in a situation where you're actually the favorite. That's always a +EV situation for you. (That's shorthand for positive expectation.)

Getting Raised on the Turn

What happens when you bet the turn and someone raises? As in our previous example, say you raise with AK before the flop. The flop comes K43, giving you top pair. You, of course, bet. When the turn brings an innocuous-seeming Deuce, you bet again, but get raised! There are a couple of possibilities to consider here.

If the raiser is a fairly passive, straightforward player, there's a good chance he flopped something strong, like a set of Fours or Threes, and was merely waiting for the double-size betting round to pound you.

If he's a loose player, another possibility is that he called your preflop raise with something puny like 65, a hand good players would routinely throw away versus a raise. If so, the Four just gave him his straight. You've shown strength throughout the hand, so it's unlikely he's bluffing.

Given how we've categorized your opponent, a fold might well be in order. But now let's say you're head-up against a loose, tricky opponent who could raise with a wide range of hands here, including many that your top pair, top kicker can beat. In that case you have an easy call and can even ponder reraising.

Folding the Turn

Even when you *aren't* raised, sometimes it's correct to call the flop, but fold the turn. Say you're dealt QJs in middle position in a $2/$4 game. You limp in and someone raises behind you. You and two others call and the flop comes AK3. It's checked to the preflop raiser and she bets. One person calls, one folds, and now it's up to you.

As it happens, you can call a single flop bet on the chance the turn will bring a Ten, giving you the nut straight. Let's do the math: eight $2 bets went into the pot before the flop (two bets from each of four players) and now two more have gone in on the flop. So you're getting 10-to-1 odds to call the $2. The four Tens you hope are in the deck give you four outs, making your odds of hitting a straight on the next card roughly 11 to 1 against. Assuming a straight will indeed be a winner, and that you'll win some additional bets if you make it, calling here has positive expectation.

Watch Your Chips

When you respond to a turn check-raise, always be sure to have a plan for the river, too. If you're calling with a hand like top pair, weak kicker, planning to fold the river if you don't improve, you may be better off to just lay your hand down now and save the bet. On the other hand, you could consider reraising with a hand like top pair with a flush draw—planning to take a free card on the river if you don't make your flush. It's also important to remember recent history—did you just fold to a turn check-raise a few hands ago? That could encourage an observant opponent into trying a bluff.

Now the turn card comes a Five. The same player bets, the other player in the hand folds, and it's up to you. This time you'll probably have to fold. True, the pot is now bigger at $26 (the $22 in previous bets plus your opponent's $4 turn bet), but the double-size bet means you're getting less than 7 to 1 pot odds. The chances of making your straight haven't improved—you're still looking at roughly 11 to 1 against. The result? Your expectation for calling has abruptly flipped from positive to negative.

While we're on the subject of odds, take a moment to glance at the odds tables in Appendix B. Get familiar with these—it'll make your turn calculations a lot easier.

On the River

Every hand is a completed hand after the fifth and final card hits the board. You know for sure what you have, but that doesn't mean playing the river is easy. You'll often face tough decisions about whether to bet, call, raise, or fold. How well you make them will have a major effect on your winnings.

Betting the River

The most important time to bet the river is when you're probably ahead. Say you have AK, there's an Ace on the board, and no likely draw. Two opponents have been calling your bets and now you wonder if you should bet your top pair, top kicker one more time. Often, you should. Players with an Ace and a worse kicker are likely to call. Even someone with a lower pair may call "just to keep you honest."

Such bets are based on the value of your hand. It may feel easier to check the river, especially since you win either way—but by failing to bet, you're failing to capture profit that should be yours.

Raise It Up

What about the times you aren't sure if you're ahead? Say you started with pocket Queens. You've been betting and by the river one stubborn caller remains. The board isn't too scary, but a King did come on the flop. It's quite possible that your opponent may have been calling along with a King and a weak kicker. But he could also have a pocket pair lower than yours, or have paired one of the other board cards. It's often better to bet again. If you check, he can bet when he does have a King—forcing you to call—but take the free showdown otherwise. When you bet, you'll still lose when he has that King, but now you can also win bets when he makes a crying call with his weaker hands.

Of course, the more opponents you have, the stronger your hand should be to bet for value. If three people have stayed to the river, one of them is likely to have top pair beaten. And if your value bet gets raised, seriously consider folding. A bluff is always theoretically possible—but bluff-raising the river doesn't happen often in low-stakes games.

 Build Your Stack _____

> Unlike the grim silence of a serious chess match, coffeehousing is a time-honored poker tradition. When a third suited card hits on the turn, your opponent might declare "I've got the flush now," while you respond, "So do I—how high is yours?" Even if neither of you really has a flush, it's considered okay by most players to misrepresent your hand. Rules and conventions regarding table talk vary from player to player and from place to place. When in doubt, we suggest erring on the side of discretion.

Folding the River

When you miss a draw to a flush or straight, you'll often have a hand that's nearly worthless and an easy fold. Likewise, when you have a so-so hand and someone bets, be inclined to fold if there are other players still to act behind you. A weaker hand is much less likely to bet, either for value or as a bluff, with many potential callers.

It's harder to fold when you have a reasonably good hand, such as two pair. But you may be wise to do so if there's a bet and a raise to you and the board makes possible a straight, flush, or full house.

Calling the River

Remember we told you to be sure and bet the river for value? Well, that's often true. But some hands are good candidates for checking the river and call-ing if your opponent bets.

There are a couple of reasons for this. First, if you're not sure about the value of your hand, it may be worth a call but not a bet, for fear of a raise—especially against a tricky player. Second, by checking in early position, you may induce a player to bluff-bet a weaker hand.

Then there's the special case of being head-up against an opponent whom you feel may have been on a draw. You won't always know by the board whether he made it or not. If he missed, he'll fold, so you won't gain anything by betting. But if he made his draw, he'll probably raise. Either way, you're better off checking and just calling if he bets hoping to catch a bluff.

Finally, there are times when the pot gets huge on early rounds and everyone but you and one or two other players fold by the river. Be inclined to call with even a slim chance of winning when the pot is big. After all, if there are 10 bets in the pot, you only have to win one time in 11 to make a call break-even.

Raising the River

The time to raise the river is almost always when you're confident of victory. That's because most opponents won't fold for one more bet, even though your raise signals to them that they're probably beat.

It's easy to raise the river when you have the nuts, or very close to it. As you improve, you'll be able to see opportunities to raise with lesser hands that are still likely winners.

Quiz on Postflop Play

Let's finish by testing your skills on each betting round:

Q: You raised to open the betting in early position before the flop with A♥ Q♥. Two middle-position players called, as did the big blind. The flop comes J♣ 8♥ 4♦, and although you were the fearsome preflop raiser, the big blind bets out. How do you respond?

A: We've started you off with a tough one! Good arguments can be made for calling, raising, or even folding.

Let's start with calling: both your cards are higher than the Jack on the board, so if your opponent only has a pair of Jacks, you'd be justified in trying to catch an Ace or Queen on the turn. Your odds of doing so are 6.8 to 1, which compares favorably to your 9-to-1 pot odds.

But what about raising? This might knock out the two players behind you, and get the big blind to check the turn so that you can see the river for free if you don't hit.

Folding becomes your best option if you're worried about a raise from one of the players behind you—especially if you fear someone has flopped a huge hand, something much better than a mere pair of Jacks.

Just to let you know, calling here is probably the right play when you're starting out, given that you have three opponents, a relatively unthreatening flop, and a bet from the first player to act. More experienced players might sometimes raise.

Q: You raise preflop in last position with two black Aces; both blinds call the raise, as do the two limpers ahead of you. The flop comes 456 with two Hearts. All check, you bet, and two players call. Now the turn adds the T♥, putting a potential flush on board. The player in first position—a quiet type—checks. The player behind her checks, too, so again you bet. Suddenly, the quiet type springs to life with a check-raise!

A: Kiss your hand and this big pot goodbye, and fold. A passive, quiet player isn't check-raising you and the other player here without the flush. Note that if she does have the flush, there is no card you can get on the river to improve to a winner. However, against an unknown or tricky player, you'd be more inclined to call, given that there are now 11 bets in the pot.

Q: You're on the river in a smallish pot. You hold QJs and the board is 2JT6K with no flush possible. Two other players are also in, and have passively called your bets on the flop and turn. Now what?

A: Go ahead and bet your pair of Jacks, Queen kicker. Sure, someone might have hit a King on the river, but it's more likely this card didn't change a thing. Anyone with a Ten will likely call you; even a hand like A6 may call. If your bet is raised by anyone who isn't a wild bluffer, you can fold in peace.

The Least You Need to Know

- How well your two hole cards "fit the flop" is a major factor in determining whether to continue—and if you *do* continue, how best to play your hand.

- Being last to act, or nearly so, is at least as big an advantage on the flop as it was pre-flop, and for the same reason: you get to see what your opponents do before they see what you do.

- On the turn, you need a strong hand or draw to continue playing, especially since in most limit games the bet doubles here.

- On the river, concentrate on capturing profit by betting or raising strong hands, cutting losses by folding weak hands, and maximizing the middle ground by knowing when to bet and when to just call with fair hands.

Chapter 6

How to Lose—and How to Win

In This Chapter

- Fixing simple mistakes with good habits
- Adjusting to the occasion
- Healing your inner poker player

Remember "Goldilocks and the Three Bears?" Well, there's more similarity than you might imagine between Goldilocks's various dilemmas and yours as you learn to play Hold'em.

Take bluffing, for example: too much can lose chips in a hurry, but too little can also cost you chips—your smarter opponents learn to quietly fold whenever you've got a big hand. Learning what's "just right" requires a lot of study and a lot of time at the tables.

Generally we learn in poker by making the wrong play, then thinking it over afterward to see what we should have done. This chapter speeds up that process with tips to help you improve your judgment and waste less time on common beginner's mistakes.

Many of these mistakes have not only a tactical or strategic component, but an emotional component as well. In such cases, it may not be enough to think in terms of mere avoidance—you need to choose an active counter-strategy. This is especially true for mistakes that are primarily emotional, and are thus the most potentially catastrophic of all to your earnings and enjoyment.

Building Good Habits

Throughout this book, we stress thinking about your responses rather than reacting automatically. However, certain things occur so often, and the speed of play is so quick, that your responses become habitual. An example is looking at your hole cards, seeing that they're trash, and flicking them into the muck.

Although this particular habit is usually fine, it's easy to form bad habits in other areas without realizing it. Replacing these with good habits takes conscious practice, but any time you can plug a *leak* by doing so, it's well worth it.

Calling Too Many Raises Before the Flop

This is an easy mistake to make—especially when you've been dutiful about throwing away trash hands and haven't seen decent-looking hole cards in a long while.

Talk Like a Texan _____

In poker, a **leak** is just what it sounds like: a bad habit or mistaken belief that's costing you chips. A good player has as few leaks as possible: she's constantly searching for ways to improve, even when she's winning. A bad player can be as full of leaks as a shower nozzle, but remain completely unaware of it. Instead, she'll blame the cards, the dealers, or the alignment of the planets—anything but her own lack of knowledge or self-control.

So what if the under-the-gun player just raised, and everyone has folded to you? You're in middle position holding Q♥J♥, and gosh, those Hearts sure look pretty! You could flop a flush draw, or a straight draw, or a full house …

This is the wrong way to think and the wrong habit to build. Over time, calling preflop raises in situations where you don't have expected value leads to exactly what you'd expect—lost chips. So instead of reacting with wishful thinking, take an extra second or two to run through your mental checklist of how to play given categories of hands.

In the example as given, you may wind up head-up with the raiser with a dominated hand. If a Queen or Jack flops, you'll be tempted to call all the way—and those times the raiser shows you the same hand on the river, but with a better kicker, will really hurt. If you were on the button with four other players having called the raiser, a call would be justified—you'd be looking to flop a draw to a big straight or flush in a huge pot.

> **Watch Your Chips**
>
> A good rule of thumb is not to call a raise before the flop with any hand you weren't thinking of raising with yourself. In the example in the text, you wouldn't have raised in middle position with Q♥J♥, so you shouldn't be calling a raise with it either. In fact, if no one else has called yet, you often need a stronger hand to call a raise than to raise in the first place!

Ignoring or Forgetting About Pot Size

This, too, is easy to do. If you're playing correctly, most of the time you're folding bad hole cards and watching others play out the hand. Who needs to keep track of the pot? You're too busy twiddling your thumbs.

But then you not only pick up a playable drawing hand, you flop an actual draw to go with it. There's a bet across the table, and you've got your chips all ready in your hand to call, when the next player in line raises! Quick—what are your pot odds? Can you call the raise or not? You don't have time to count the jumbled pile of chips, so you hastily call or fold, unsure in either case of whether you did the right thing.

Avoid this scenario by drilling yourself repetitively: any time you're not in the pot, count those chips as the players put forward their individual bets or raises, until it's a habit you can count on.

As a side note, another advantage to not looking at your hole cards until it's your turn to act is that you can pick up *tells*, while avoiding giving any tells yourself. See Chapter 8 for more on this subject.

Raise It Up

Don't try to count the pot by counting the actual dollars—not only is this hard to do, but when it comes time to figure your pot odds, you'll have to expend extra effort dividing the pot size by the bet size in dollars. For limit poker, it's a lot easier to count the pot by how many bets go in it. This also makes your pot odds easier to figure, because you're always dividing by bets, not dollar amounts.

Adjusting to Fit Your Opponents

Hold'em doesn't reward a one-size-fits-all strategy. One type of opponent may doggedly see the river with 90 percent of his cards, rarely if ever raising; another may raise frequently but fold even more frequently when raised back. If you play these two types the same way, you'll lose.

You'll learn more about this notion of varying your play in Chapter 8. For now, the following sections outline two basic categories of mistakes that can be corrected by equally basic adjustments.

Bluffing Too Much, or Not at All

We've already said that in low-limit Hold'em, most of your opponents err by calling too much. This type of player is a *calling station*—someone you can count on for a lot of profit whenever you have a strong hand and he's got a weak one.

However, if you insist on bluffing calling stations, the advantage shifts to them: in effect, they are now using the correct strategy by calling your poorly considered bluffs.

Another beginner's mistake is to bluff in multi-way pots, especially on the river. If it's hard to bluff one typical low-limit player, imagine how hard it is to bluff three or four!

But what if you never bluff, meaning that you only bet or raise with your good hands? In a typical low-limit game, that's not nearly as costly a mistake as bluffing too much. Still, as we've already noted, decent players will pick up on this and stop calling whenever you start betting—unless they themselves hold an extremely strong hand—one that could likely beat you.

The cure isn't to start bluffing with any old hand, but to learn an advanced technique called *semi-bluffing*. This involves bluffing with a bet or raise when you don't yet have a hand, but have at least some chance of making a good hand on the next card. We'll explain this technique in Chapter 8, so stick around.

Keeping Everyone Honest, or Folding at the Drop of a Hat

Both of these are unrewarding extremes. As an example of the first, if you find yourself in the habit of glumly calling along when you have a fair hand, while knowing in your heart you're beaten, you may have morphed into a calling station.

It's a matter of judgment, because folding a hand that could have scooped an entire pot is a far greater error than losing an extra bet or two. But if you consistently find yourself staring at better hands at the showdown, you've acquired a leak that you need to correct.

Start by getting rid of the notion that you have to call to "keep players honest." The idea behind this adage is that it's a sin to let anyone win a pot by bluffing. The problem is, this doesn't take into account whom you're calling.

If that fellow who calls along to the river with 90 percent of his hands suddenly starts betting, the chances are excellent he's not bluffing. Even with players you know to be habitual bluffers, you're better off calling them only with your fair hands, not with just any old hand. You're not calling "to keep them honest," you're calling only when your hand has a good enough chance of winning in relation to the size of the pot that you'll show a long-term profit.

Here's a good rule of thumb: if you *never* get bluffed out of a pot, it's almost certain you're calling too much.

The other extreme is getting so snake-bitten that you fold your fair hands whenever someone raises, or in some cases, reraises. This is especially a problem when you're head-up against an aggressive player. If he sees that you habitually give his raises too much respect by folding all but your very best hands, he may start raising with nothing. This is called *running over* someone who's playing *weak-tight*.

Against such a player, you'll have to call more often than you might prefer. You don't have to *always* call—just often enough that he knows he can't count on disposing of you as easily as that.

 Talk Like a Texan _____

A player who folds too readily, or who only bets his very strong hands while playing tightly and passively otherwise, is said to be **weak-tight**. This is one of the worst insults one poker buff can hurl at another. On the other hand, many poker experts contend that learning how to play weak-tight is the first step toward playing well, since it means you are at least being selective about which hands to play.

Handling Emotion

One of the ironies of Hold'em is that we spend all this time learning highly rational strategies, when the game itself inspires the most irrational of behaviors. This is to our advantage when other people behave irrationally, but alas, few of us are free from the same curse.

Broadly speaking, letting emotion influence you is called being on *tilt*, or *tilting*. The term presumably comes from pinball: ram a pinball machine too hard with your hip, and the machine shuts down and you lose.

Tilt comes in many forms and just about every Hold'em player has fallen victim to it more than once—even seasoned pros. We'll look first at a fairly subtle example, one that many players wouldn't even recognize as tilt unless they thought about it. After that, we'll examine tilt's broader effects on nearly every aspect of play, along with what you can do about it.

Hanging On to Big Pairs with a Death Grip

Say you raise preflop with a pair of black Aces and get several callers. The flop comes T♥9♥8♣, so you bet with confidence. To your surprise, a normally timid player raises and a third player calls. You reraise and both players call. The turn adds another Heart. The flop raiser bets again, but this time, the third player raises! What to do?

If you're like most beginners, you're so loath to fold your overpair that you call both the raise and the reraise, and perhaps, another raise and reraise on the river. The first raiser shows a set of Tens, whereupon the second raiser shows the King-Queen of Hearts for the flush and takes all the chips. You sit there mumbling to yourself about Aces being a terrible hand. The problem here isn't that you truly believe Aces can never lose; it's that you're overly attached to them. And attachment, as practitioners of Buddhism would be quick to remind us, is an emotional response. Therefore, when you call down in this sort of situation, you've let emotion get the better of you.

This specific instance of tilt has a fairly easy remedy: learn to recognize that a big pair is just another Hold'em hand. Your goal is to play all your hands as well as possible. You should eventually be able to let go of pocket Aces that you recognize to be losing just as easily as you'd throw away any other losing hand.

Tilting Full-Blown at Any Windmill

In its most nefarious forms, tilt has you charging hard at everything, winning nothing. Let's say you suffer a *bad beat* when your set of Jacks is drawn out by a player who makes a straight, but who you feel isn't justified in calling your preflop raise with his horrible cards.

Talk Like a Texan

A **bad beat** occurs when you've got a strong hand that you're playing correctly, only to lose to an opponent who played poorly but overtook you. An example might be when you raise preflop with AK, make top pair on the flop, but lose to someone who makes an improbable two pair with a hand like 82s—a hand he probably shouldn't have called your pre-flop raise with. Although some players use the term to refer to any particularly dismaying loss, this is incorrect.

You are furious. Without realizing it, you start playing hands you'd normally throw away. You start bluffing calling stations, something you never do. And on and on it goes. You are on tilt.

This is an extreme example, but unfortunately a very common one. Even when you're not actually angry, nearly any emotion at all can hurt your play. If you feel great about having just scooped a pot, you may loosen up and start playing any two cards, believing that you're on a roll.

Or let's say you take another bad beat, but this time, instead of loosening up, you do the reverse— you tighten up and start throwing away decent hands you'd normally play for a small profit. Smart opponents, recognizing what's happening to you, may take advantage by running you over with bluffs.

How to combat tilt? Like everything else, it takes practice, but here's some ideas to get you started:

- **Be aware of your emotions as you play.** An easy way to do this is to pause occasionally in the moment before it's your turn to act. Use that extra second or two to check in on your feelings.

- **Think about how you'd play if you weren't feeling this way.** For example, if you sense you're about to raise out of anger or a desire for revenge, take an extra moment to consider how you'd play your hand if you *weren't* so angry.

- **Take frequent breaks.** Whether you're playing at a casino or online, there's no rule that says you have to stay at the table, playing hand after hand while you're in a rage. Get up, walk around, go for a stroll. If you're playing with a buddy, talk over how you're feeling and how you're playing.

- **Concentrate on playing your best, not on winning or losing.** It's a strange thing, but the more desperately you want to win chips, the worse you'll probably play. Conversely, the less attention you pay to how you're doing, the more you can focus on playing each hand well. You'll learn more about this approach in Chapter 11.

- **Remember that past events don't affect the next hand.** You'll hear players say a seat is cold, or that they never win against a certain other player or with a certain hand.

Don't let their superstition infect you! You know full well that the cards you get are random and that the odds don't change because you're ahead or behind. If you flip a coin 10 times, you might flip seven heads and three tails. That doesn't change the fact that it's still a 50-50 proposition on the next flip.

- **Have a fall-back strategy.** We've warned against changing your strategy when you're shaken up—and we've also warned that you may be better off taking a break or even quitting for the day. But if you insist on continuing to play, tightening up is far better than loosening up. For example, it wouldn't be terrible to play only your very best starting hands for a while. The idea is to avoid having to make difficult decisions until you regain confidence.

The Least You Need to Know

- Avoid mistakes such as forgetting the pot size by developing good Hold'em habits—for example, by practicing counting the pot when you're not in hands.

- When it comes to questions such as when to bluff, when to call, and when to fold, avoid extremes such as "never" and "always"; instead, make your decision based on your opponent and the situation.

- To keep tilt at bay, practice counter-strategies such as monitoring your feelings, taking breaks, and concentrating on playing your best rather than winning chips.

Chapter 7

Online, or Bricks and Mortar?

In This Chapter

- Casino and club checklist
- Online play checklist
- Playing shorthanded
- Cheating and other chicanery

So far, most of this book teaches you *how* to play Hold'em. In this chapter we look at *where* to play, and for what stakes. There are more choices than ever before—from Internet sites to casinos, and from penny stakes to big bucks.

For pros, online poker offers a vast selection of games and the ability to play multiple tables at once. Although it's almost impossible to make a living playing a single $3/$6 game, playing four or more such games simultaneously is a different matter. For amateurs who are just starting out, the main advantages to online play are convenience and the ability to play for ultra-low stakes.

But playing live has attractions, too. If you work in front of a monitor all day, you may prefer to see other people or feel the buzz that permeates most cardrooms. You're more likely to strike up actual friendships with fellow players in a cardroom than chatting online. And only in live play can you eventually learn to spot *tells*—those giveaway behaviors or facial expressions that reveal what an opponent really thinks of his hand.

Just as e-mail hasn't eliminated the need for face-to-face contact, the boom in online poker hasn't dented live Hold'em venues. In fact, cardrooms and casinos are booming, and the legions of players who learned the game online are most likely one reason why.

Casino and Club Checklist

If you decide to give live play a try, call the nearest casinos or cardrooms and ask what stakes they offer. Generally, the lowest limits are $2/$4 or $3/$6, although a few casinos do spread $1/$2 structured limit and $1/$3 spread limit. When you arrive, look for a list of games currently available. In small clubs, it may just be a clipboard; in casinos, it's likely to be a big board showing games, stakes, and the initials of waiting players. Ask for your game of choice. If there's a free seat, you'll be directed to the table. If not, your initials will go on the waiting list.

Raise It Up _____

As you gain experience and skill, there's one crucial factor to consider in choosing your table: locating a **good game.** In poker terms, that means a game where at least one or two of the players are terrible, and where overall you'll be one of the better players. As a general guideline, look for loose games with lots of callers, little raising, and a generally happy mood. It pays to be choosy. Even the tenth-best Hold'em player in the world won't do too well at a table with the top nine.

Rules and Etiquette

Here are a few basics to get you ready:

- **Buy-in amount:** Hold'em games usually have a minimum buy-in. For a $2/$4 game, it might be as little as $20. However, we recommend buying in for 30 big bets—in this case, $120. That gives you enough ammo to last a while. You can get chips at the cashier or at the table, depending on cardroom policy.

- **Posting:** When you first sit down, you'll generally have two choices: either "post" the amount of the big blind and get cards right away, or wait until it's your turn to be big blind. If there are only a few hands to go, it's generally more economical to wait.

- **Table stakes:** You can only bet money you have on the table in the form of chips and cash—reaching into your wallet isn't allowed until the hand is over. It's frustrating to finally get a good hand and be unable to win the maximum—another good reason to buy-in for more than the minimum.

- **Betting:** It's important to wait your turn to call, bet, raise, or fold. It's not just good manners—acting out of turn can wreak havoc. Some players may change their minds about betting or calling and others might be irritated if your error interferes with whatever action they were planning. Do your best, but don't worry too much if you slip up a few times: part of the dealer's job is to help newcomers understand what's required.

- **Raising:** If you want to raise, be sure to put the full amount out all at once. Don't place enough to call in front of you and then return to your stack to raise. That's a string bet, and will usually be disallowed. It's a good idea to announce what you're doing each time you act: "Bet," "Call," and so on.

- **Looking at your hand:** Look at your cards by separating them slightly and bending them up at one corner, shielding them with your free hand. And never pick up your cards and hold them outside the table's edge—not only is this against the rules in most cardrooms, but it can make it easier for other players to see them.

Talk Like a Texan

When everyone folds to the blinds, they can opt either to play the hand out, or chop by taking back their blind bets. In many low-stakes games, the house takes a cut of the pot if a flop is dealt, but not on a chop. That's a pretty powerful point in favor of chopping, but it's always your call. Chopping is a convention, not a rule. Whatever you do, be consistent. Chopping your weak hands but playing your monsters is widely considered as taking unfair advantage.

- **Protecting your hand:** We mentioned this back in Chapter 2, but it bears repeating: if your hole cards get mixed up with other cards on the table, or if the dealer thinks you've folded and mucks your cards, you're out. As a safeguard, place a chip, coin, or trinket on top of your cards.

- **Declaring your hand:** When two or more players reach a showdown, the last bettor or raiser is required to show his hand first. If at that point you're certain you've lost, it's fine to toss your cards into the muck and keep your own secrets. But if you *aren't* 100 percent sure, go ahead and turn your hand up so the dealer can declare the winner. Even veterans sometimes miss an unlikely straight, flush, or other winning hand.

- **Tipping:** When you win a hand, it's customary to tip the dealer: like waiters, dealers depend on tips for much of their income. At low limits, $1 is usually plenty, although if you win an especially big pot you might make it $2 or more. When you take a tiny pot, it's fine to skip the tip. In cardrooms where dealers get to keep their own tips rather than pool them, we're inclined to be more generous with fast, efficient dealers. And if a dealer is slow, rude, or mistake-prone, you needn't tip at all.

- **Customer service:** The *floor* isn't just what you walk on in a cardroom—it's also a catch-all title for middle management. If there's a dispute between players or you want to change tables, you need to call the floor.

Online Checklist

Some things are the same online as live, such as posting blinds and table stakes. Others simply don't apply—betting and raising are done by clicking a mouse, and you don't tip the tiny robot dealer inside the software.

Rules and Etiquette

One big difference in online play is that you can't just plunk down cash in exchange for chips. Before beginning, you'll have to get funds into an account at your chosen poker site. We strongly recommend choosing one of the biggest and best-known sites. At this writing, the authors both play primarily on Party Poker (we have no other relationship with the site, and simply offer it as an example).

Here's our logic: a company spending millions on marketing—and making billions in rake—has a strong business motive in protecting its customers. That's important, because a player would have little legal recourse against a fly-by-night site that misused financial information, tolerated cheating, or refused to pay out winnings.

Most major credit card companies won't allow gambling transactions, nor will some online intermediaries. If you're comfortable giving a site your bank account information, you may be able to make a direct electronic transfer. But even if you're playing at a well-known site, we recommend you find a reputable online payment firm to act as middleman for the transaction. If all else fails, you can always mail a bank check or postal money order.

After you've funded your account and are ready to play, here are some useful things to know:

- **Finding a game:** Internet poker software typically lists games in progress. When you find a game at your stakes, just click and you'll be taken to the table.

- **Taking notes:** Almost all online sites let you take electronic notes on other players, which goes a long way toward compensating for the fact that you can't see your opponents. Notes let you keep track of your adversaries' individual quirks and betting habits. And the very act of taking them keeps you attentive, even when you're not in a hand.

- **Regulation:** Unlike U.S. casinos, which are almost universally subject to gaming commissions, tribal authorities, or other regulatory bodies, online poker sites exist in a shadow world. Running one is illegal in the United States, and all the major sites are operated offshore. Despite this, the large sites have a solid reputation for running honest games, with attention to customer service and no problems cashing out.

Raise It Up

The rake is the house share of each pot. A typical rake in a live $2/$4 game might be $2 on the flop, a dollar more when the pot reaches $20, and a final dollar at $30. That's a lot of money coming off the table every hand, and a good reason to move up to slightly higher stakes when you can: the rake is often the same dollar amount in the bigger game, and therefore, a smaller percentage. Rakes are generally lower online than live, perhaps due to the faster rate of play and lower overhead.

Playing with Fewer Opponents

Most of the strategy advice in this book has assumed you're sitting at a full table of seven to nine players. But what if it's shorthanded? This happens in lulls at cardrooms, at the final table in tournaments, and online, where special tables offer seating for five or at most six players. Many players aren't comfortable shorthanded, but if you make the right adjustments, it can be both fun and profitable.

High Cards Go Up in Value

With fewer hands dealt, normally weak hands like AT and KJ become relative powerhouses. Draws, on the other hand, become traps: with a hand like T9s, you want at least three callers to get the right odds, and you'll seldom get this many shorthanded.

Aggression Pays

Forceful play pays off shorthanded, so if you're first in, knock the door down with a raise. Many pots are contested head-up or three-way, and the winner tends to be whoever bets first. Unlike full games, where someone usually has a hand, shorthanded play is about winning lots of small pots with weaker holdings. If you're head-up or against just two opponents, however, it pays to vary your style fairly often—for example, by switching from super-aggressive to moderately conservative. Then, just before your opponents catch on, switch the other way again.

Playing Multiple Tables

Who says there's nothing new under the sun? Until the advent of the Internet, it was unheard of to play more than one game at once. Now it's the norm for many online players to play two, three, four, or even more tables simultaneously. The obvious advantage is the potential to multiply your hourly profit; the disadvantage is the increased chance you'll play poorly for lack of concentration.

Keeping Track of the Action

When you first play online, it's probably best to stick to one table. The pace of play is faster than a live game (no shuffling or other delays), and at first can be overwhelming. After you get comfortable, you can try adding a second game, and see if you can handle the distraction. Chances are, you'll find it's not that hard—and you may even enjoy the accelerated pace. Playing more tables means you'll have a good hand somewhat more often, and that can actually improve your discipline.

How Many Is Too Many?

We've found that playing two or three tables at once keeps us from getting bored, without being overwhelming. But it's common for small-stakes professionals to play four tables, and some reportedly play as many as eight tables at once! Dedicated multi-tablers often invest in oversized monitors, so multiple tables are onscreen with no overlap. If you decide to try multi-tabling, you'll probably want to experiment. If you feel you're not making good decisions, you can always cut back.

 Build Your Stack

Multi-tabling has created an entirely new species of poker pro. The prototype is a young, male math whiz, although we know of successful older and women players as well. The best of these new professionals are able to make six-figure incomes playing anywhere from one to eight tables for stakes ranging from $2/$4 into the thousands of dollars. Many invest in multiple monitors to let them view all their tables at once. While it's hard to see this as a long-term career path, it's also hard to see why a 20-something earning $150,000 a year playing Hold'em online would quit to take up a $35,000 a year job in the "real" world.

Cheating and Other Bad Behavior

If you're playing in a reputable casino or cardroom or on a well-known Internet site, cheating almost certainly won't happen often enough to affect your results. If you do suspect something, don't be shy—report it to the powers that be. You'll be protecting other players besides yourself.

Collusion

Probably the most common form of cheating occurs when two or more players team up. They can *jam* the pot when one of them has a strong hand, extracting the maximum from anyone trapped in the middle, or use multiple raises to force others to fold.

Colluders don't necessarily make out all that well, though. For one thing, they risk multiplying their losses when an intended victim has a strong hand. For another, collusion can be spotted relatively easily: the operators of online sites can review hands played by players under suspicion. So colluders are taking a real risk of being caught and banned.

Marked Cards

Sometimes players bend or otherwise mark a card so they can spot it later. The cards now used in most public cardrooms are made of tough plastic, so it isn't easy to do. You might be more likely to run into this in a home game. That's also where you might see simple cheating tactics, such as importing extra chips into a game or hiding an Ace.

Angleshooting

Much more common than outright cheating is *angleshooting*—tricks and ploys that are unethical, but not clearly against the rules. Again, if someone persists in angleshooting, don't hesitate to complain to management.

Here are a few common ploys and ways to defend against them:

- **Lying about a hand:** At showdown, some players will say they have a flush or straight when they really don't. Or they may ask if you can beat a particular hand. They're hoping you'll muck, giving them the pot. The solution is simple: protect your cards until they show theirs and the dealer declares their hand.

- **Shorting the pot:** Some players deliberately put in too few chips, "forget" to put in a bet, or raise or even slip chips out of the pot. The dealer should keep this behavior in check, but if you're at a wild table, keep your eyes open.

- **Peeking at other players' cards:** Knowing another player's hand gives the angleshooter an unfair advantage not only over that player, but over everyone else in the game. It's perfectly acceptable to ask the victim to protect his cards.

- **Acting out of turn:** Some players check or even show their hands before you have a chance to bet, hoping for a free card or showdown. If you want to bet, firmly assert that you hadn't yet acted and stick to your guns.

- **Deliberately timing out online:** If your Internet connection goes down while you're in a hand, most sites don't fold your virtual cards, but allow you to win that part of the pot you contributed to, should your hand prove best at showdown. Some players take advantage of this safeguard by disconnecting on purpose, to see a showdown without having to call any more bets. There's not much you can do about this, but fortunately the major sites generally limit players to two or three disconnects per day.

The Least You Need to Know

- Places to play Hold'em include casinos, cardrooms, and Internet sites.

- Online play offers convenience, low stakes while you're learning, and the chance to play multiple tables simultaneously if you get more serious. Live play lets you see opponents, meet other players, and enjoy the ambiance of the cardroom.

- To beat shorthanded games, get aggressive with your weaker big-card hands while playing fewer draws.

- Although most players and games are on the level, cheating and unethical behavior do occur. Generally a little alertness and common sense are all it takes to protect yourself.

Chapter

Advanced Lessons

In This Chapter

- Introducing the semi-bluff
- Common types of players
- Common types of games
- Hand-reading and tells

The basics we've laid out so far are the foundation for Hold'em success. A good handle on starting hands, pot and card odds, and fundamental strategy will help you at least break even in most low-limit games. But we want you to do much better than break even, so we're taking your education to the next level with some advanced strategies.

If you're brand new to Hold'em, some of this material will probably feel overwhelming. That's okay—you'll work with these concepts for as long as you play poker. There's plenty of time to learn their nuances as you gain experience.

Semi-Bluffing Gives You Two Ways to Win

When you bet with what you think is the best hand, you're trying to win money from players who call. And when you bluff, you're trying to win the whole pot by getting everyone to fold. But what if you bluff with a hand that could also win?

If that doesn't make sense, consider a situation like the following: preflop, everyone folds to the dealer; he raises, the small blind folds, and you call in the big blind with a fairly weak hand, T9s. You know there's a good chance the dealer is trying to steal here, opening so late. The other thing you know about him is that he's aggressive, but not very imaginative.

The flop comes 278, giving you a straight draw. The flop is small enough that if he holds a bare Ace, or two big cards such as KJ, he's now got next to nada.

This is a great spot to consider a check-raise. If you check on the flop, most players will bet with any hand. This sets you up to represent a strong hand with your check-raise, such as A8 for top pair plus top kicker, 87 for two pair, or a set of Deuces.

This kind of play is a classic *semi-bluff*. Notice that you've got two ways to win here: first, if he indeed holds a weak hand like Ace-high, he may fold outright—even AK won't look as strong to him after you check-raise. This lets you win a pot that in most cases would have been his if he'd called you down. Second, even if he goes ahead and calls, you still have better than a 1-in-3 chance of making your straight and beating him by the river.

Sure, you might make the same play with no draw at all, on a pure bluff. But because the semi-bluff has greater expectation, you can semi-bluff much more often than you can bluff, and with greater confidence. You can raise where some players would just call, and bet where they would check. Your opponents will have a harder time reading your hand and be less likely to bluff into you, knowing you're more likely to *play back* than other players.

Talk Like a Texan

Smart, aggressive players often **play back** by raising or reraising head-up, especially when they smell a bluff or a steal attempt. Usually they play back when they have outs—meaning their raise or reraise is a semi-bluff with some chance of actually winning. A passive player, by contrast, seldom plays back—he's happy to fold if he doesn't hold a definite hand.

Semi-bluffs are most often employed against just one opponent. And usually they involve hands like straights or flushes, as we've seen. But any play at all where you bet, raise, or check-raise with a hand that can improve to win is considered a semi-bluff, as long as there's some chance your opponent may fold.

Keep in mind that the more likely an opponent is to fold, the less of a hand you need to semi-bluff with; the more likely he is to call, the better your hand should be.

Raise It Up

Comments along the lines of "How could you play that way?!" are common at the table. When you're the target, you may be tempted to set the record straight by reciting your outs or the odds the pot was offering you. Don't! Instead, ignore the question, or answer with a joke or polite evasion.

Who Are These Guys?

Hold'em would be very dull (and very expensive) if your opponents played perfectly. Fortunately, most of them will make lots of mistakes, usually centering around their style of play—for example, too passive, too loose, or both. Here's a look at the most common types of players you'll encounter:

- **Les Gamble.** Les is *loose-aggressive*—he likes to raise and bluff a lot. It's good to have Les seated to your right, so you can see his bets coming. When you think you have him beat, you can take advantage by raising to pressure players with so-so hands or draws. Les bets his strong hands, his medium hands, and sometimes his weak hands, too. So you're going to have to call him more, especially when you're head-up.

- **Loose Lucy.** Lucy is *loose-passive*, donating freely by calling with any hand at all and rarely betting or raising. When she *does* come to life with a bet or raise, she's usually got a very big hand—so you don't have to call unless you've got a monster yourself. Be sure to bet for value against her, but don't bother to bluff; Lucy lives to call you down.

- **Slippery Sal.** Sal is loose, too, but he's also tricky. He plays hands such as 56s and J3s and has been known to call three bets pre-flop with 22. Although bad habits like these make him a long-term loser, Sal does have good card sense. He's capable of strong plays such as semi-bluff raising on the turn. And the wide range of hole cards he'll play make it hard to know which cards help him. Sal is aware of how opponents play, so you'll need to consider what he thinks of you. For example, if you've folded a hand or two to raises, it's more likely he'll try a bluff if the two of you are head-up.

- **Earnest Reader.** Ernie, as his friends call him, knows how to play *tight*—at least when he first sits down. He's fresh out of college, has read some poker books, and wants to play the "right" way. But in the heat of battle, he sometimes slips and plays more like Les or Lucy than the expert he hopes to become. Watch the size of Ernie's stack, and his mood as the game progresses, and adjust your calling and raising requirements against him accordingly.

- **Weak Willie.** Willie is *weak-tight*: afraid of the nuts! If a flush or straight is possible, he's sure someone must have it. He'll tend to fold all but his best hands to a bet or raise, regardless of pot odds or whether he's head-up. Willie isn't around as much as he used to be these days, except at the very lowest limits. Players like Les and Sal are just too hard for him to beat. When you do encounter Willie, you can bluff more and fold weak hands with confidence if he fires back.

- **Mr. and Ms. Chips.** You guessed it—these are the folks who neither call too much, nor fold too often. They patiently wait for good hole cards and adjust their play, depending on opponents, pot odds, and card odds. Just like the other players we've described, they make mistakes and have losing nights. But unlike the others, they've also got the know-how to win more often than not—and to keep improving. You want to *be* Mr. or Ms. Chips, not play against them.

What Kind of Game Is This?

When you put 10 players around a table, their different playing styles combine to give the game a *texture*, as it's called in poker parlance. Smart players adjust to different games; bad players never adjust.

Let's look at some common types of games. As we do, keep in mind that, like the imaginary players we just discussed, these games are stereotypes. In real life, you need to play each hand on a case-by-case basis. For example, even the loosest tables have an occasional head-up pot. And remember, too, that in a crowded cardroom (or online site) with players coming and going, a table can undergo dramatic mood swings in the course of a few hands.

Loose-Aggressive Tables

Put a couple of raise-happy opponents at the same table and rock'em, sock'em action is likely to follow. It's not uncommon to have raises and reraises before and on the flop, with the action slowing on the turn and river.

Tighten Up Before the Flop ...

You need to be extra selective about starting hands in a very aggressive game—folding more draws up front than usual. Drawing hands play well when you can get in cheaply and see if the flop will help. In an aggressive game, where the pot is constantly getting raised and reraised, it's often too expensive up front to make drawing hands a good investment.

In early to middle position, you'll prefer premium hands, such as 99 and higher for pocket pairs, along with big suited cards, such as KQs and higher. These all play well in raised pots. If you're in late position, though, you *can* sometimes add drawing hands against just one raise—but only if other callers are already in, and if you don't expect the pot to get jammed behind you. These extra hands include JTs (but no lower) and all the smaller pairs, from pocket Deuces through pocket Eights.

... and Loosen Up After

With so many players calling two or more bets preflop, the pot will be big enough that you can pursue many hands you'd normally throw away—inside straight draws, overcards, even middle or bottom pair.

For example, say you hold JTs and end up seeing the flop with five other players for a bet and a raise. The flop comes 38Q, giving you an inside straight draw. It's checked to the button; he bets, gets two callers, and it's your turn. Normally you'd fold, but here you've got an easy call: with four Nines to give you the nut straight, your odds to see the turn are 11 to 1, and the pot is offering you better than that at 15 to 1.

Or say you were the preflop raiser with AK on that same flop. Your odds of hitting an Ace or King on the next card are about 7.5 to 1—so you could call a bet and even a raise here. Moreover, you could even bet out here yourself, on the slim possibility that everyone missed this ragged flop. (Remember semi-bluffing?)

In a loose-aggressive game, the big pots and ups
and downs can make you feel as though you're on
a rollercoaster. Stay patient, and concentrate on
keeping the odds in your favor. You can be losing
after hours of frustrating folds and missed draws,
then become a big winner by dragging one or two
huge pots.

Loose-Passive Tables

When four or more players routinely see the flop
without a raise, it's an invitation to play many more
drawing hands than usual. You can safely limp baby
pairs and small-suited connectors even under the
gun, knowing you'll usually get lots of limpers
behind you and no raise. Most of the time you'll
miss the flop and quietly fold. But those times you
connect, you'll generally get plenty of calls and win
a fair-size pot.

The Odds Favor Draws ...

Let's say it's a $2/$4 game, and you limp in with
pocket Deuces against five opponents. Your
chances of flopping a set are about 8 to 1 against,
while your immediate pot odds are only 5 to 1.
But you also need to consider your "implied odds,"
additional bets you can win if you hit your hand:

> We can hypothesize that three of your oppo-
> nents will call a $2 bet on the flop if a Deuce
> does fall; two will likely call a $4 turn bet; and
> at least one will call the $4 river bet. That
> works out to 14 to 1 odds on your $2 initial

bet. Here's another way to look at this: seven times you won't hit a set and you'll fold, losing $2 each time for a total of negative $14. The eighth time, you'll hit your set and hopefully win $28 or more. If you do the math as discussed in Chapter 3, it works out to a positive expectation of at least $1.24 every time you limp those Deuces.

Of course, it isn't that simple. Sometimes there'll be a raise behind you and you'll pay more to see the flop. About 20 percent of the time you'll hit your set and lose anyway. All this chips away at your expectation—but you're still getting the best of it when you can come in cheaply with hands like these.

Talk Like a Texan

A **fish** refers to an unskilled, losing Hold'em player. The more the game you're in resembles an aquarium, the better for you in the long run. When the fish are schooling, though, the short run can be frustrating. In a game full of piscine players, there's always a good chance someone will take down your AK with K2 when the flop comes K22. Just remember, the guy playing K2 against AK is going to get filleted more often than not.

... But Big Cards Win Less Often

A penalty for getting a crack at so many cheap draws is that your very best starting hands will lose more often than in a tighter game. For example, you can raise with AA, get five callers, and lose when some *fish* who called your raise with K7s makes a flush, or a hand like 54 makes two pair.

Does that mean you shouldn't raise your big pairs? Absolutely not. You'll win less often, but you'll still be a money favorite. For example, if you raise with AA and get five callers to the flop, you've contributed less than 17 percent to the pot—but your Aces are a favorite to win a third of the time or more. We'll take those odds whenever we can get them!

What's more, you don't always have to call to the end with your big pair—when you play awhile, you'll learn to recognize lost causes and fold accordingly. For example, if you hold A♦A♥, the flop comes 89T with all Clubs, and there's a bet and a raise, you can usually fold. This goes back to the idea of reverse implied odds in Chapter 3: even if your opponents haven't flopped a straight or flush outright, they've got too many ways of beating you, and you've got hardly any ways to improve to beat them.

Should you still raise before the flop with offsuit big-card hands such as AK, AQ, and AJ? Yes with AK, but not always with AQ or AJ. If six limpers have entered the pot and you're on the button with AQ, it's fine to keep the pot smaller by just calling, and then waiting to see if you flop good.

Tight-Passive Tables

It's unusual to find a very tight low-limit Hold'em table—playing too many hands seems to be a more common mistake than playing too few. But tight tables are out there, and you can do very well against a bunch of tight types as long as they also play fairly passively.

With fewer opponents than usual, drawing hands go down in value and high cards go up. The semi-bluff is also more valuable. When you're the first player in, you can raise preflop in middle position with terribly weak hands such as 44 or A9s. If you're first in from late position, you can raise with as little as K10 or A5.

In this manner, you can run over the game by winning lots of small pots. It's easy to bluff if the other players only call or raise when they have strong hands.

Tight-Aggressive Tables

When play at a table is tight but aggressive, it's much harder to win. Now lots of pots will be played head-up or three-way, but the players will semi-bluff their draws, slow-play big hands, value bet into your draws, and play back at you when they think you're bluffing.

In short, tight-aggressive tables aren't very profitable because the other players are playing too well. Your best strategy when you find yourself at a table like this: look for a better game.

Hand-Reading and Tells

By combining general knowledge about a player with the board and the action, you can often read the hands he's likely to be holding.

Example 1

You raise preflop with J♣J♠ in middle position. Les Gamble and Loose Lucy both call. Now the flop comes A♦4♦5♣. You bet, Les raises, and Lucy calls. You also call. The turn card is the 2♦. You check, Les bets, Lucy raises.

Knowledge of your opponents tells you this is an easy fold. Although Les is capable of betting without an Ace, Lucy almost certainly wouldn't raise without the goods—probably either two Diamonds for the flush, or even a trey for the straight. She's a loose player, and it's perfectly possible she called your preflop raise with a hand like 8♦Q♦ or 33.

Example 2

Slippery Sal limps and you raise on the button holding A9. Earnest Reader calls in the big blind and Sal calls, too. The flop comes 10♠9♥5♠; Ernie checks, and Sal bets. You raise as a semi-bluff with what may or may not be the best hand, and although Ernie folds, Sal calls. The turn card is the 6♣; Sal checks and calls your bet. The river brings the 2♦, and Sal again checks to you. What's your move?

This time, your knowledge of Sal and your read of the action suggests putting in one more bet. Being aggressive, Sal wouldn't have passed up a check-raise on the turn if he had a big hand—so there's a good chance he's gotten trapped with something relatively weak. Maybe he's got two Spades and will simply fold to your bet. Maybe he has a hand like 10♦ 8♦ and will call and beat you. But there's also a good chance he's holding a little pair like 44, suited cards like J♠ 6♠ that missed the flush but paired on the turn, or even two overcards. When that's the case, he often calls and you collect an extra bet.

What Are the Players Telling You?

If you've seen the movie *Rounders*, you probably remember the scene where Matt Damon's Mike McDermott picks up a tell on his primary opponent, Teddy KGB. Teddy likes to eat Oreos while he plays high-stakes Hold'em, and Mike notices he only eats the cream when he has something strong. By observing this cookie tell, Mike avoids a heavy loss with a well-timed fold.

Watching for giveaway actions like this can help you, too, but not as often as you might think. If you're playing online, tells are pretty much non-existent. And in live games, you won't always know whether a stranger's shaking hand is due to excitement, age, or too much coffee.

Still, there are many common tells worth knowing about. Here are a few examples:

- When the flop is dealt, most players will watch the cards. Watch their faces instead. A player who glances quickly from the board to her chips may have hit something strong. A player who continues staring at the board may be disappointed by what he sees.

- Occasionally you can detect an impending bet or raise by watching for naïve players who unconsciously pick up chips before the action gets to them. Some players grab chips anytime they intend to call. Watch until you know who's who and what their habits are.

- Body language can speak volumes. For example, if someone who was slumping sits up a little straighter when he sees the flop, something good has probably happened for his hand. But such body language should be subtle: anything blatant is usually an act put on for your benefit.

- A player who talks to an opponent after betting may be trying to coax him into calling.

The Least You Need to Know

- A semi-bluff gives you two ways to win: one if everyone folds, the other if you're called and your hand improves enough to take the pot.

- By categorizing opponents along the lines of loose, tight, passive, or aggressive, you can more easily profit from their errors.

- Hand-reading is the skill of figuring out a range of likely hole cards for an opponent based on her playing style, the betting action, and the board.

Chapter 9

Introduction to No-Limit

In This Chapter

- Cash games versus tournaments
- Key differences between no-limit and limit
- Small-stack strategy for beginners
- Common mistakes to avoid

The champion frowns at the flop. After a brooding pause, he detaches three monster stacks of chips and pushes them gently forward, using just his fingertips. The challenger, a much younger man, bounces nervously in his seat—then with a sweeping gesture pushes his entire stack into the pot.

That's right—it's no-limit Hold'em, and our hero has just gone all-in. If the champion calls, they'll both flip up their hands. As the crowd holds its breath, the dealer will burn and turn the final two community cards before declaring the winner.

You just don't get that kind of rush in limit poker. That may be one reason why no-limit is such a natural for television and the movies. It also helps explain the craze for easily affordable no-limit tournaments and *cash games* online and in cardrooms over the last few years.

Talk Like a Texan _____

> You may have noticed that we haven't used the term **cash game** up until now. That's because all regular poker games *are* cash games, whether played at home or in public cardrooms. The only reason to use the term is to draw a distinction between tournament and non-tournament play.

In case our example didn't make it clear, in no-limit you can bet any number of chips, up to everything you have on the table. Success under these conditions requires an oversized heart, a nitrogen-cooled computer for a brain, and Svengali-like skills at mind-reading and manipulation—all of which explains why Doyle Brunson once described the game as "the Cadillac of poker."

Even for ordinary mortals, though, no-limit can be lots of fun. As with all poker, the key is to build your skills while sticking to stakes you're comfortable with.

No-limit is such a different cat from limit that we're actually going to cover it in two chapters. In this chapter, we'll introduce key differences between no-limit and limit Hold'em, along with basic no-limit skills—the essentials you'll need to start playing in small cash games. In Chapter 10, we'll explore the additional skills required for tournament play.

Considerations for Getting Started

We'll look at no-limit techniques shortly. But first, let's talk about a couple of important considerations that affect how to go about learning this game.

Cash Is King

If you've been weaned on the World Series of Poker or the World Poker Tour, you may so completely associate no-limit with a tournament setting that you can't imagine playing it any other way—even if you've never played it at all. As you'll learn in the next chapter, however, tournaments require you to master not just one, but several different strategies, as you scramble to keep pace with ever-increasing blinds and ever-shrinking hand values. If you're just starting out, you're more apt to get killed than educated.

In cash games, by contrast, the blinds stay the same, making it easy to practice basic moves and slowly extend your repertoire. The best beginner strategy is to play very tight, with super-solid hand values. This is much how you'd play in the opening stages of a large tournament. After you get experience, you can then experiment with playing more loosely—just as you would in the *later* stages of the same tournament.

You'll soon discover that cash game play is incredibly fun and complex in and of itself. Some of the toughest cash game players don't play in tournaments at all, yet they still get great respect from their peers.

Ratcheting Down Your Buy-In

Being able to commit to that all-in push when it's the right move is an absolute must in no-limit. That means you'll want to play with a smaller buy-in than you're used to in limit Hold'em. If you play super-tight, as we recommend for beginners, you should be playing with a small buy-in anyway; this keeps you from having to make a lot of tricky decisions. Big stacks allow more room for creative play, but you're not ready for that yet.

Even with a small stack, you can still buy plenty of time at the table. Typically, the blinds are quite small in a no-limit game, making it easy to keep folding while you wait for good cards. And most games feature limits on the minimum and maximum buy-ins. These limits place a ceiling on the typical pot size, allowing a small stack to compete before the flop with much bigger stacks.

Just to give you an idea, a typical *baby no-limit* game features blinds of $1/$2, a minimum buy-in of $40, and a maximum buy-in of $100. The comparable limit game in terms of what you can win and lose is somewhere around $5/$10, with blinds of $3/$5. You could buy-in for the $40 minimum in the no-limit game with no problem, but you'd need a minimum of $250 to sit down in the limit game and feel you could last awhile.

Finding a Cheap Classroom

Where can you find no-limit games that are fun, instructive, and affordable? One good place is online: today, you can easily find games featuring blinds as small as 25¢ and 50¢, with a maximum buy-in of $25. As for live play, many casinos and cardrooms now feature the baby no-limit games already mentioned.

Regardless of the venue, one danger for raw novices is repeatedly getting broke and buying back in, too dazzled to realize how quickly your cash is draining away. Try to limit yourself to a maximum of two or three buy-ins per session—that way you'll absorb more from your table time than just a pounding.

> **Talk Like a Texan**
>
> To **get broke** in a no-limit cash game is to lose all your chips. That's different from a tournament, where the same unfortunate situation is called **busting out**. And please note that because in poker we talk like cowboys or grifters, "get broken" ain't correct—it really *is* "get broke."

Key Differences Between Limit and No-Limit Hold'em

A good way to approach no-limit is to compare it to limit Hold'em and see how things differ. Obviously you compute your odds in the same way, so what's changed?

- Certain categories of hands that are merely strong in limit become monsters in no-limit. These include sets, straights, and nut flushes. Ideally an opponent won't realize how strong you are, and will commit all his chips with a good but inferior hand, such as top pair, two pair, and so on.

- Other categories of hands become much weaker. These include AQ, KQ, and so on—fine in limit for making top pair with an okay kicker, but trouble in a no-limit cash game. You *can* open with these hands in late position, but in a cash game you almost never want to back them with all your chips. (Tournaments are a different matter.)

- Position becomes critical, especially when combined with the power of the bluff. Strong players use position to bully a weak game with monster bets and raises, forcing the players who've already acted to guess whether the strong player has a killer hand or two bad cards. Guess wrong, and there goes your stack! Brunson once wrote that if he could always have position in no-limit, he'd win every hand, regardless of his cards.

Why Doyle Carries a Big Stick

Traditionally, an expert no-limit player sitting in a cash game prefers to have the biggest stack at the table—in no-limit parlance, he wants to have everyone else *covered*. There are three reasons why:

- The bigger your stack, the more money you can potentially win. For example, say your opponent has $500 and you've got only $60: if you get all-in against him, the most you can possibly win is $60, *doubling up* your chips. But if you had a $150 stack, you could win $150 in the exact same situation.

- A big stack is better for inducing fear. This is especially true when you've got position on your opponent. He could bet out—but you might then raise him all-in. He could check, but that might give you a free card that beats him. And so on, and so forth. His thoughts work against him, where they wouldn't if your stack was smaller than his and you couldn't put him in such jeopardy.

● A big stack can let you play more speculative hands than you could otherwise. This typically applies if you're up against opponents who play certain kinds of hands poorly. If you read an opponent for a hand like pocket Aces, but he fails to raise enough before the flop, you can correctly draw to hands like small straights and flushes. You know that if you make your hand on the flop or turn, there's a good chance your foe will donate his entire stack rather than surrender.

Raise It Up

In limit Hold'em, you commonly get the right pot and implied odds to draw on the flop and turn to straights and flushes. This lets you play hands like JTs, A3s, and so on. But in no-limit, drawing hands in raised pots often get no better than 2 to 1 pot odds on the flop. That means you should rarely play them in aggressive cash games.

The exception is if you're up against loose, passive opponents who fail to raise enough preflop to protect hands like big pairs or AK. The rule of thumb is that if their preflop raise is no more than 5 percent or so of your stack, you can profitably call with a drawing hand. Your implied odds come from the fact that if you flop good, you'll have a shot at their entire stack.

Why You'll Be Starting Small

All of this is great fun. But because this is a beginner book, we're not going to teach you how to play a big stack. Big stacks demand skill in reading opponents and skill in bluffing; without those skills, a big stack just makes you a big target. A small stack is easier to play, more affordable while you learn, and still gives you an excellent chance of winning. Your profits won't depend on bluffing, but on getting called.

In most beginner-level cash games, the blinds will be small enough relative to even a small stack that you can sit back and wait for premium hands—typically pocket pairs 99 and higher, AK and AKs, and sometimes AQs. You'll raise just enough preflop to get calls from one or two players with weaker hands—Aces with bad kickers, smaller pocket pairs, two high-suited cards, and even worse. These speculative hands won't be getting the implied odds they require, but your opponents won't notice a detail like that.

If you like the flop, you'll be aiming to push the rest of your stack in then and there. Big-stack players won't be able to bluff or intimidate you, and players who foolishly called your preflop with weak hands won't have the pot or implied odds to continue. That's why a small-stack strategy is simple—and effective.

Small-Stack Strategy in Detail

Here are the nuts and bolts of playing a small stack, from buying in to pushing in.

Buying In

We'll use the example of a baby no-limit cash game with $1/$2 blinds, a minimum buy-in of $40, and a maximum buy-in of $100. You'll buy in for the minimum of $40, of course—but notice that even this amount is still 20 times the big blind. That gives you ample room to patiently fold bad hands while you wait for good ones. If you get blinded down too far, just rebuy to get back up to $40.

Hands to Play

Early Position	Middle Position	Late Position
TT and up, AK	99 and up, AK	77 and up, ATs
AKs	AQs and up	AJ and up, KQ

Here are some observations on specific hands:

QQ, KK, and AA: These hands aren't just for raising, they're for reraising. JJ by contrast is much less of an automatic reraise: head-up against AK or AQ, Jacks are slightly better than even money; against QQ, KK, or AA, they're a 4.5 to 1 underdog.

Pocket pairs TT and smaller: The smaller the pocket pair, the more you want to cut the field to a single opponent, if possible—or even steal the blinds, in late position. Unless you flop a set, there are too many overcards that can come on the flop to beat you to feel comfortable in a multiway pot.

AK and AKs: The primary function of Big Slick is to get head-up against an opponent with a weaker Ace—or to induce everyone to fold to a hefty reraise preflop, allowing you to win without show-ing down. AKs is a better hand than AK only because of its potential to flop the nut flush draw—or even better, the nut flush draw plus top pair, top kicker.

AQ, AJ, KQ: These hands play far more weakly in no-limit than in limit; they generally flop no better than top pair, and they're dominated by AK. KQ in particular has the reek of day-old fish; you can open with it as dealer, but only barely. Never call a raise with it.

Sizing Your Preflop Raise

Unless you're in the blinds, you'll pretty much never just limp in. Instead, you'll raise or reraise. You don't want to raise so much that everyone folds, nor do you want to raise so little that every-one calls. You want one or two callers, hopefully with weaker hands than your premium hand.

A typical opening raise is from 3 to 4 times the big blind—in this case, from $6 to $8. But that will vary, depending on the following factors:

Have other players already limped into the pot ahead of you? In that case, you'll likely need to raise more to discourage a crowd.

Is the game extremely loose? Again, you'll probably have to raise more than usual, perhaps as much as 5 to 6 times the big blind.

Has someone already raised in front of you? If you choose to play rather than fold, you'll want to size your reraise so it gets you head-up with the initial raiser.

Are you opening the pot on the button? The temptation is to put in a very small raise rather than fold the blinds, but this is a mistake. Trying to trap in this fashion is a good way to lose your chips to a garbage hand that flops lucky. You're always better off forcing the blinds to define their hands rather than see a cheap flop.

What If You Get Reraised?

If someone reraises behind you, or if a limper who just called ahead of you now decides to reraise, your choice of action will depend on two things: your estimate as to what hand he might hold, and the size of your remaining stack relative to the pot.

Estimating the strength of your opponent's hand always involves some guesswork, but your accuracy will improve with experience. In some cases, the reraiser may be trying to knock out other players and get head-up with you, which likely indicates he holds a strong hand himself; in other cases, the reraiser may be trying to steal the pot without a fight, figuring your small stack means you'll play more conservatively than usual.

If you've already committed half your stack or more to the pot, there's hardly any hand you should fold to a reraise; you're better off calling or raising all-in. A quick example shows why this is correct:

> Say you pick up pocket Jacks at a point where your small stack has been blinded down to just $30. The table has been playing quite loose, so you raise $15 after two limpers in an effort to narrow the field.

> The blinds fold, the first limper folds, but the second limper reraises you all-in. There's now $45 in the pot and it will cost your remaining $15 to call. If you had x-ray vision and could be certain the raiser held a bigger pair than your Jacks, your 3 to 1 pot odds wouldn't be enough to call. But what if he's holding AK or AKs, making you a slight favorite, or a pair smaller than Jacks, making you a 4 to 1 favorite instead of a 4 to 1 underdog? Factor in all these scenarios, and you've got an easy call.

Raise It Up

In limit Hold'em, you're almost never all-in before the flop, whereas in no-limit, it's a common scenario: one player raises preflop, another reraises, and the first pushes all-in, daring the second to match him.

Because of this, you've got to know an additional set of odds: how different kinds of hands typically fare against each other head-up to the river. These are called **race odds**. For example, any bigger pair is more than a 4 to 1 favorite against a smaller pair; any small pair is a 6 to 5 favorite over AK; and so on. For more race odds, see Appendix B.

On the Flop

There is no formula for playing the flop, even with a small stack. Sometimes you'll have the luxury of position, but often you won't. You'll have to learn how to interpret your opponents' actions in a no-limit setting, taking into account their playing tendencies, what they think of your tendencies, and the texture of the flop. Here are some typical scenarios:

> **Small flop.** Two players limp, you raise, and the flop comes with three small cards—no picture cards and no Ace. If you've got an

overpair to the board, you're probably in good shape. One of the limpers may bet into you as a probe, hoping you raised with two big cards; he may even have a genuine hand, such as a small set—though in that case he'd be more likely to slowplay. Unless you have a clear read that he's super-strong, be prepared to go all-in here.

Flush-draw flop. If the flop comes with two of a suit and you don't have a flush draw yourself, there's a good chance someone may make a play at you, whether or not he's actually got the draw. Again, if you have an overpair, your goal here is to cripple drawing hands by over-betting the pot or going all-in. Sometimes you'll lose when a player makes his draw, but more often you'll win.

Overcards. You raise with a medium-big pocket pair such as Jacks or Queens, and the flop comes with an Ace—or worse yet, with an Ace and a King. The Ace is a scarier card for you than the King, as many loose players will call almost any preflop raise holding an Ace and a small card, whereas they'll let go of a King and a small card in a hurry. If you're first to act, bet somewhere between half to the full size of the pot, and see what happens; if you're last to act, you'll have to size up the action ahead of you before committing yourself.

On the Turn

You'll rarely reach the turn playing a small stack, but most of the advice for the flop applies here as well. So long as the turn card and the action seem to indicate you're still in the lead, you'll want to push the rest of your stack in if it isn't already. After that, sit back and wait for the smoke to clear on the river.

Beginner Mistakes to Avoid

Watching a baby no-limit game is like watching beginners ice skate: most of the time, everyone is falling down. Try to avoid making these common mistakes yourself, while staying alert to see who among your opponents makes them:

Limping in as opposed to raising preflop. It's typical in these small games to see family pots in which *everyone* limps in, hoping to hit big flops with junk. If you see this happening, be prepared to win some money—as long as you avoid the habit yourself.

Trying to bluff loose players who've caught a piece of the board. You want to bluff tight players who think; loose players are apt to call you down with surprisingly weak hands.

Calling big bets by passive opponents who show signs of excitement. After you learn to read players in no-limit, you realize that many of your opponents won't commit sizeable money to the pot unless they have a huge hand. Unless you've got a monster yourself, or have an unmistakable tell that they're bluffing, you've got no excuse for paying them off.

Calibrating your preflop raises to the strength of your hand. With a small stack, this is less of an error than with a big stack—but it's still a bad idea. If you're first in the pot, don't raise more with pocket Aces just because they're Aces, and less with pocket Jacks just because they're Jacks. That's giving away too much information.

Underbetting the flop. Another trait you'll see quite often in bad players is raising with a big pair or two big cards before the flop, then getting scared on the flop and putting in a pea-sized bet—say, a quarter or a third of the pot. This just gives loose players the odds they need to continue and draw out on you. Even if you raised with AK and completely missed the flop, you'll usually want to bet from one-half to the full size of the pot, assuming you have position and no one else has shown strength.

Calling and hoping. If you find yourself in the position of always checking and calling, not betting or raising, something's gone wrong. You won't show a profit in no-limit until you learn to apply pressure like a 300-pound masseuse.

Refusing to let go of a big overpair when the action indicates you're beat. Again, this is less of an issue with your small stack, but it's still something to be wary of. Say you raise preflop on the button with pocket Aces and get just one caller, a very loose player who limped in ahead of you and who loves to play drawing hands. The board comes 789 and he quickly looks away—an unmistakable tell that he's hit a big hand. He checks, you bet the pot, he raises you all-in. In limit Hold'em, you'd never fold your Aces here; but in no-limit, your decision will rest in part on the size of your remaining stack. The bigger your stack, the worse Aces will perform for you—but that's getting into big-stack play, which we can't cover here in detail.

Cash-Game Quiz

All these problems assume you're playing a loose $1/$2 game, with $45 of chips in your stack.

Q: You open-raise to $8 on the button with AQ; both blinds call. They're loose players with big stacks, and often call raises together, apparently for the pleasure of playing against each other. The flop comes A25, giving you top pair, pretty good kicker. Both blinds check; you bet $15, about two-thirds of the $24 pot, and get called in both places. The pot is now $69. The turn comes a Four, seemingly not a scary card for you; you're ready to go all-in with your remaining $22, but to your surprise, the small blind now bets the pot. To the small blind's surprise, the big blind raises him all-in. Do you call all-in, or fold?

A: Fold. The big blind almost certainly has turned a small straight; there's a good chance the small blind has a straight also. Even if the river gods brought a Five, letting you play the board, you still might lose if one of the blinds holds a Six—quite possible if they're really loose. If the board were slightly less scary, however, you'd be better off calling: there would be too good a chance you'd have both the blinds beat, especially if you sensed that one of them was trying to steal the pot.

Q: In middle position you pick up AQ of Spades after two loose limpers. You put in a $12 raise; the dealer calls, the big blind calls, and so do both of the limpers. The pot is now $60. The flop comes Q♥8♠3♠, giving you top pair, top kicker with the nut flush draw. The first limper bets $10, a tiny raise given the size of the pot; the second limper folds, and it's to you. Should you just call in hopes of sucking in the blinds, knowing you can make a big move on the turn?

A: In a limit game it might make sense to wait until the turn to raise, but not in no-limit—especially given that the pot is far bigger than your remaining stack. You may be up against a small or medium set, a worse Queen, or a worse flush draw; regardless, your all-in bet will surely get called. Get your money in now; you're probably either winning or in an excellent position to pick up the win by making your flush.

Q: The under-the-gun player limps in; he's been playing quiet and tight, despite the $250 stack he's sitting on. You're next in line; you tease up the corners of your cards and glimpse red pocket Tens.

You raise to $10; everyone folds to the button. He too has a stack of more than $200, and now he uses some of it to raise to $30. You're thinking about pushing all-in ... when the under-the-gun player announces he's reraising to a cool $80. What the heck is going on?

A: We don't know what the button has, but almost certainly the under-the-gun has Aces or Kings; the limp followed by an all-you-can-eat reraise makes this clear. If you call all-in and the button also calls, you'll be getting pot odds of 2 to 1 at best, and you're worse than a 4 to 1 dog here. Fold and watch the fireworks.

The Least You Need to Know

- Pot odds generally tighten up in no-limit. This means loose, passive play is even less successful than in limit Hold'em.

- A small-stack strategy lets you back hands like top pair, top kicker, and overpairs with all your chips and show a profit against loose players.

- Bigger stacks prefer hands like flushes, straights, and sets, since these hands can break opponents who overplay top pair.

- With any size stack, success at no-limit depends on playing the bully rather than submitting to being bullied.

Tournament Tips and Tactics

In This Chapter

- What makes tournaments different
- Fundamental concepts
- Basic beginner strategies
- Tournament types

Probably no form of Hold'em has grown faster than tournaments. The first World Series of Poker (WSOP) back in 1970 was contested by just seven players, whereas the WSOP main event in 2005 drew 5,619 entries.

And that's just the tip of the chip stack. Small, medium, and large buy-in events have become wildly popular both in casinos and online, while televised poker is pretty much all tournaments, all the time.

Why are tournaments so attractive to so many players? For one thing, your risk is limited to your buy-in. For small tournaments, this amount is often quite affordable. For another, that buy-in gives you a chance to win a vastly larger sum. It's like entering a lottery, except this lottery involves skill as well as luck.

What Makes Tournaments Different

Much of the strategy you'll use in tournament play is the same as that for a cash game—but there are three key differences.

Difference #1: Fixed Number of Chips

In tournaments, everyone buys in for the same amount and gets the same amount of chips in return. These chips have mock dollar values that apply only to the tournament. Except in tournaments that allow rebuys (a subject we'll touch on later), you can't buy more if you go broke.

This restriction makes for extreme strategy changes, depending on the stage of the tournament and how close you are to elimination. Sometimes you'll hoard your chips as long as possible; other times, you'll look for any excuse to attack.

Difference #2: Rising Blinds

In cash games, the blinds don't change. But in tournaments, they start small and get bigger at set intervals. For example, in a $50 buy-in tournament where each player gets 500 in chips, the blinds might start at $5/$10 and move up from there, perhaps doubling every 10 hands. The idea is that rising blinds force the action, keeping players from just sitting on their chips waiting for premium hands hour after hour. In later stages, antes may be added as well to further juice the pot.

Raise It Up

Tournaments put such heat on players that tells begin to spring up like beads of sweat. Ever see a player in a televised tournament talk to an opponent who's just gone all-in? He's trying to get a tell before he decides whether to call. Maybe the opponent's voice cracks, or maybe he squirms when he should stay still. You can also watch for betting patterns, such as betting more with strong hands than with weak ones, or for how a player handles his chips when he's bluffing versus when he has a real hand.

In the early going, when blinds are low, you'll generally want to play tight. Let the other players fight for the lead and knock each other out. The more players who bust out early, the fewer you'll have to battle later. As the blinds rise, you'll be forced to mix it up more. You do this by trying to steal small pots wherever possible, in addition to jamming with any quality hands you manage to catch.

By the time you reach the final table, the blinds often get so big in relation to your stack that you may have to go all-in on any moderately good hand, such as A8, 67s, or 33.

Other players will be feeling the same pressure, and may raise or call a raise with weak cards or on a bluff. Unless you've got a huge chip lead, survival becomes a matter of stealing blinds, pushing weaker holdings, picking off bluffs, and being lucky enough to win a few showdowns at the right time.

Difference #3: Prize Structure

As we mentioned earlier, your goal isn't to win chips; it's to place as high as possible in the tournament. It used to be that almost all skilled tournament players played tight in the early and middle stages. This way they could see a lot of flops cheaply, while looking for opportunities to outplay opponents at minimal risk. Not until the final table would they be willing to push all-in and go for broke.

But today, some of the most successful young tournament players follow a different strategy. These young guns are much more willing to risk busting out early, in exchange for a chance to build up a big stack and bully their way into the money.

These younger players have grasped an essential tournament truth: the point is to shoot for the prize pool, not for mere survival. In a tournament that pays prizes to only the final 10 players, finishing eleventh pays the same as finishing last.

Build Your Stack _____

Most tournaments allow players at the final table to make a deal dividing up the prize pool; this allows the chip leaders to avoid the risks involved in duking it out to the last hand. But since everyone's cooperation is required, a player with a small stack can often negotiate for a bigger cut, in exchange for not blocking the deal. Feared players can do the same: in their case, they're auctioning off the chance they might outplay their opponents if things continued.

Tournament Paradoxes

If you haven't played tournaments before, the following observations may seem weird. As you gain experience, though, you'll see they're completely logical.

The fewer chips you have, the more value each chip has. Let's say a tournament comes down to you and two opponents. They each have $24,000 in tournament chips, but you have just $2,000. The prize structure, meanwhile, is $1,600 for first place, $800 for second, and $400 for third. Even though you only have 4 percent of the chips, you're guaranteed to win at least 14.3 percent of the money!

Sometimes it's best to fold a great hand. Say only the top seven finishers get prize money, and there are eight players left. You and one other player are the smallest stacks at the table. On the next hand, she goes all-in, but gets called by a big stack in late position.

Sitting in the big blind, you glance down at your cards and find pocket Queens. In a cash game, you might push all-in too—but this is a tournament. You realize that if your Queens fail to hold up, you'll bust out in eighth place and win precisely nothing. Your best move is probably to fold and hope the big stack wins the confrontation with the all-in player. That way, *she'll* bust out in eighth place, and you'll have edged into the money.

Watch Your Chips

Always know how the prize pool is structured. In the 2002 World Series of Poker, finishing first paid $2,000,000, second $1,000,000, and third more than $500,000. However, places 6 through 9 paid much less, from $150,000 down to just $85,000. It's no surprise that play at the final table was conservative, as players tried to outlast one another to reach the far more lucrative prizes near the top of the pool.

Small stacks must be gamblers to stay alive. You might think that conservative play is correct with a small stack—but actually, it's the reverse. Any time your stack drops to five times or less than the blinds, you've got to get super-aggressive rather than let yourself be blinded down to nothing.

You'll have to move in with any decent hand—even if you're opening in late position with hands you'd normally consider indecent.

"Decent" here can mean a small pocket pair, suited connectors, or a bare Ace. Indecent can mean something as bad as K4 if you're opening in the cutoff or as the dealer (ouch!). If you steal the blinds, great! If you get called with a reasonable hand, or even with your King-high garbage, you've still got a chance to win and improve your standing relative to other small stacks.

Raise It Up

A quick way to measure your position in a tournament is to see how many rounds your stack is worth. For example, with blinds at 100 and 200, a 3,000 chip stack is worth 10 rounds of play. A huge stack would be 30 rounds or more worth of chips. A large stack would be 10 to 30 rounds, a medium stack would be 4 to 10 rounds, and a small stack would be enough for just 3 or fewer rounds.

With a huge stack, you can obviously afford to wait for good hands. With a small one, you'll have to be ready to go all-in at the drop of an Ace. In between, you'll need to use your judgment. In general, you'll be more aggressive (and less selective) as your stack dwindles relative to the cost of a round.

A Basic Beginner Strategy

So how do you start playing tournaments? An obvious piece of advice is to start small. Maybe it's a $5 buy-in, single table tournament online, a Saturday afternoon event at your local casino, or an invitation to a friendly home tournament.

Regardless, you'll want a basic strategy to get you as deep into the event as possible, without having to know a lot of subtle moves. That's what we present here. Even these highly abbreviated guidelines may seem a lot to remember when you're just starting out, so pay attention!

Early Rounds

At the start, you'll almost always have a huge stack relative to the sum of the blinds. We advise that you play just two hands: AA and KK. That's right, you're only going to gamble with the best two hands in Hold'em! As you get better, you'll be adding other hands and trying to build your stack right from the start. But for now, you're just going to play pocket Aces and pocket Kings.

In early position, or later in a pot where no one else is in, you'll want to raise about 15 percent to 20 percent of your stack before the flop. For example, if you have 1,000 chips, a raise of 150 to 200 would be correct. That's enough to give anyone with a draw or underpair the wrong odds to call and try to hit a straight, flush, or set. If one or more people are already in the pot, you'll want to bet even more. If the total pot is already more than half your stack, just go all-in.

If you're called, you're almost always going to put the rest of your money in on the flop. There are two exceptions, though. The first is when you have pocket Kings and an Ace flops. If your opponent puts in a bet of any size, play it safe and fold. If no one bets, go ahead and bet anywhere from half to three-quarters of the pot. If you get called, check the turn. You'd like to see a showdown, but you'll have to fold if your opponent bets. With the blinds still small relative to stack sizes, you're trying to build your stack, not get busted.

The other time to be wary is when the flop comes without an Ace, but your opponent goes all-in before you can bet. Here you'll have to use judg- ment. On a board like Q98, many players will go all-in with a hand like AQ—which you are well ahead of. On the other hand, a more conservative opponent, wary of your big preflop raise, might need a real monster to push, like a set of Nines or JT for the straight. When in doubt, fold and live on to see another flop.

Middle and Late Rounds

As the tournament progresses and the sum of the blinds and antes increases relative to your stack, you need to expand your hand selection. You also need to get more aggressive, because winning the blinds is now worth more.

With a huge or merely big stack, you'll still stick to opening only with AA and KK in early position, raising about 15 to 20 percent of your stack. But in middle position, you can now open with a few additional hands: AKs, AK, and QQ, as well. Rather than just raise a percentage of your stack with these additional hands, go ahead and push all-in. If you're the cutoff or button and no one has limped in, you can push in with pocket Sevens through Jacks, or with AQs. When opening in the small blind, add KQs down through 54s, pocket pairs from Deuces through Sixes, and any suited Ace. Again, push all-in with these lesser hands.

The same basic strategy applies with a middle-sized or small stack, but you'll be going all-in with the lesser hands in earlier position. With a mid-sized stack, you can go all-in with AA-66, AK-ATs, and AK-AQ in early position. Opening in middle position, you can add the suited connectors and pocket Fives or Fours; opening in late position, you can add pocket Deuces and any suited Ace. Typically you'll be pushing all-in with these lesser hands, especially if your stack is small.

If other players have already entered the pot, things get trickier. If there's a big raise in front of you, you'll want to pull way back with a big stack; you're in no rush to get into a confrontation. That means folding everything except AA-QQ and AKs or AK. (If the raiser is very loose and aggressive, you can loosen up.) With a medium stack, you'll probably want to get your money in with JJ-99 as well. With a small stack, you'll want to throw away suited connectors and Aces with kickers below a Ten, but push in with AJ or better or with any pair.

Raise It Up

Always try to keep your stack size big enough to make calling an all-in bet on your part painful for opponents. For example, if the average chip stack in the middle stages of a tournament is $2,000 and you're down to $500 in chips, with the blinds at $75 and $150, you need to try and double up fast. If you don't, the next round of blinds will shrink your stack to just $275, making it easy for multiple opponents to call an all-in bet.

Final Table

By the time you make it to the final table, or to one of the final three spots in a single-table tournament, the blinds will have grown to the point that they'll dent even huge stacks. That means it's time to strap on even more aggression than before.

For the purposes of this section, we'll assume six or fewer players remain. If there are more, keep following the middle- and late-round guidelines.

With fewer players, you can basically play as if you were in middle position or late position all the time. Go all-in with pocket Aces through Sixes,

AKs through ATs, AK, and AQ, but fold all else. If there's a limper in front of you, only go all-in with pocket Nines or better, AKs, or AK.

With three players left at the table, your list of all-in hands now includes all the above, plus pocket Fives through Deuces, 54s through KQs, and any Ace. There's one exception, however: if a player has already gone all-in and gotten called, you'll usually want to avoid getting involved without a monster hand—pocket Queens through Aces, AK, or AKs. Remember, folding here gives you a chance to grab at least second place without risking a thing.

Finally, if you make it to head-up play, we recommend you simply go all-in every hand. Subtle it's not, but you've got a 50-50 chance of being ahead in any given hand. The high blinds will force your opponent to either let you take his money without a fight, or get in and gamble with you. You've effectively taken any extra skill he might have out of the equation, making luck and nerve all that matter.

From Grade School to Graduate School

Our beginner's strategy is admittedly a blunt instrument. If you find you like tournaments, you'll want to develop additional skills, such as reading opponents and playing speculative hands when conditions permit. Some excellent books on no-limit in general and tournaments in particular have been published in the last couple of years; see Appendix C for our recommendations.

Tournament Types

If you want to play in the World Championship Event at the World Series of Poker, you'll have to come up with $10,000 for the buy-in. At the other end of the financial spectrum there are tournaments online you can play for $5 or less.

You probably don't need help choosing the right buy-in size, but tournament structures can vary almost as widely as the stakes. Here's a quick guide to help you sort out the choices.

Build Your Stack

The most famous no-limit tournament is the so-called World Championship, the centerpiece of the annual World Series of Poker. The first championship was actually made up of a rotation of five games, including no-limit Hold'em, with Texas legend Johnny Moss declared the winner by vote of the players. The next year, 1971, the championship event was restricted to just no-limit Hold'em. Only five players competed, and Moss won again. The championship has grown a bit since then: in 2005, there were 5,619 entrants, and champion Joseph Hachem won $7,500,000.

No-Limit Tournaments

This is the type of multi-table tournament we've been discussing so far, with rising blinds and pay-out amounts based on the total entry fees minus the sponsor's fee. Typically, everyone at the final table finishes in the money, with first and second place earning the lion's share. At huge tournaments like the WSOP main event, even a fiftieth place finish can be rewarded with a five-figure payout.

Rebuy Tournaments

In addition to the initial buy-in, many tournaments allow rebuys—purchases of additional chips during the first half-hour or hour of play. Some tournaments limit how many rebuys you can make, while others permit unlimited rebuys.

In most tournaments, additional chips cost the same as the original buy-in. Rebuys are therefore only a bargain if they'll make a real difference. For example, if a lot of players were knocked out early and you've managed to accumulate a medium-size stack, it may be worthwhile to rebuy, because your chances of winning have improved considerably.

Satellites

Eric Drache, who ran the World Series of Poker for many years, is credited with having invented smaller "satellite" tournaments in the early 1980s, to expand the field for the main event. The idea was that a satellite could charge a few dozen players

$500 each and award a $10,000 seat in the World Series of Poker to the winner. That gave players who couldn't afford the usual 10 grand buy-in a shot at the championship for a bargain price.

Recently, online poker sites have taken this concept even further. With thousands of players participating, satellite entry fees are frequently less than $50. In fact, 2003 WSOP main event champion Chris Moneymaker won his seat online, in a $40 satellite event.

Sit and Go's

These one-table events are sometimes offered live but are especially popular online, where the buy-in can range from $5 to $25 per player. As the name suggests, after the table is full, the tournament begins. They're a good way to get a feel for tournament play without investing a lot of time or money. Fewer entrants increase your chances of finishing in the money, but, of course, they also decrease the amount you can win.

Shootouts

These are multi-table tournaments with a twist. In a normal tournament, as players get knocked out, the survivors are reseated so that tables are always as full as possible. But in a shootout, players stay at their initial table until a single winner emerges victorious. The individual winners from each table then convene on the final table to thrash it out.

Limit Tournaments

In limit Hold'em tournaments, both blinds and betting limits rise. The steady increases have the same effect on strategy as in a no-limit tournament, forcing the action and increasing the tension between those players with tall stacks and those with short ones.

There's even less reason to mix it up early on in a limit tournament, because you can't trap someone for his or her whole stack. It's worth chipping away in the middle stages, though, in hopes of building up a stack that will give you staying power when bet sizes get truly outlandish later on.

The Least You Need to Know

- Tournaments are distinguished by three key characteristics: your chips are limited and you can't buy more; the blinds keep rising; and you're playing for a share of the prize pool, not the chips on the table.

- Tournaments force you to alternate between extreme aggression and extreme conservation, as you balance hoarding irreplaceable chips with building a big stack and busting opponents.

- A wide range of tournament sizes and structures are available. In all cases, it's essential to know the number of entrants, the blind structure, the prize pool structure, and whether rebuys are allowed.

Chapter

Having Fun Without Going Broke

In This Chapter

- Variance and bankrolls
- Keeping poker in perspective
- Going pro—is it for you?

After seeing your share of flops and raking in a pot or two on the river, you'll likely come to a decision about whether Hold'em is the game for you.

Like golf, chess, and other recreational pursuits, Hold'em can be a lifetime source of pleasure and intellectual stimulation. In this chapter, we offer a few final tips to help you get the most out of the game, while avoiding frustration and disappointment. You should know that even for the best of players, poker is a bumpy ride. Understanding the statistical reasons for this can help make your own ups and downs easier to handle.

Such knowledge helps in other ways, too. Specifically, you'll be better equipped to decide how much money to commit to the game and what sort of stakes to play for. In effect, you're in charge of your own poker economy.

A Random Look at Results

When you're first learning, you expect to lose most of the time. But you may be under the impression that after you get your game together, you'll start winning steadily and never look back.

Unfortunately, that's not how poker works. Even the best players can—and often do—suffer losing streaks that last for days, weeks, or months. And although it's rare for a solid player to endure a losing streak of a year or more, it's statistically possible.

This has to do with what's generally called *variance*. This is a statistical term that means that any series of results with a random component to them will tend to be scattered above and below their long-term average. In the case of poker, although we know that probabilities apply in the long run, the cards are most assuredly random in the short run.

Moreover, the better you get as a player, the bigger your variance. Why? Because you're sitting there waiting for occasions when you have positive expectation. And each time you find one, you're committing as much money as you can by raising, semi-bluffing, and so on. In the long run, this is smart, but in the short run, your results depend on fewer and more heavily weighted events. It's like you're driving on a washboard dirt road leading to a gold mine, but in an old pickup with no shocks. You'll get the gold, but not without some bumps and bruises along the way.

Watch Your Chips

Hold'em hands are just a series of random events. How you play them is anything but random. It's human nature to try to make sense of our experiences—most of us only have to touch a hot stove once (at most) to learn it hurts. Getting AKs cracked hurts, too. But don't let that stop you from raising the next time you're dealt it! While bad beats are a fact of life at the table, bad play doesn't have to be.

In contrast, many bad players are loose-passive, committing relatively small sums of money to many events—basically, calling with many hands and rarely raising. This results in a nice, smooth pattern of results, like gliding down the road in a fine limousine. Of course, it's also a *losing* pattern, so the limo's destination is not a gold mine, but a cheap motel with no running water and a broken color TV.

Fighting Back with Record-Keeping

What can you do to tame variance? First, and perhaps most essential, you need to find out if you're a winning player. You do this by keeping detailed records of every session you play. The essential data to record are location, stakes, session length in hours, and your dollar wins and losses. You can do this in a small notebook or however you like. Later, you may want to transfer this information to a spreadsheet to make calculations easier, but that's not a requirement.

After you accumulate enough data, you can start analyzing your performance. How much data is enough? Generally, a couple hundred hours is best, but you can begin calculating before that to get practice. What you're working out is your *hourly rate*—the average amount you win or lose for each hour you play.

Assuming you're playing limit poker, you can take a further step by dividing your hourly rate in dollars by the big bet for the stakes you're playing at. This gives you your hourly rate in big bets per hour. It's handy as a measure of how well you're doing compared to how well you *could* be doing. Basically, if you're beating a limit Hold'em game for one big bet or more, you're on your way to becoming a winning player.

But what if you find you're *not* a winning player— that even after you learn the game and put in some time studying and playing, you seem to be consistently losing or at best struggling to break even? Here are some suggestions:

- Play for the smallest stakes possible. Not only will you stand to lose less, but you'll be up against softer competition—so you have a better chance to start winning.

- Purchase the practice software listed in Appendix C and confine yourself to battling computerized opponents. When you can beat the machine, you'll be ready for live play again.

- Investigate online poker forums (also described in Appendix C), where you can post sample hands and get a critique of your mistakes.

- Talk over your play with a friend, if possible. There's nothing like having to explain your strategy to bring mistakes to light.

- Rethink your goals. There's no shame in breaking even or losing small amounts if you can afford it. After all, people commonly set aside money for hobbies they enjoy.

- If you find yourself losing more than you can afford, or stealing time from other commitments to play Hold'em, seek help. Gambler's Anonymous, individual counseling, or trusted friends are all viable alternatives.

Build Your Stack

> Even the best players don't do much better than one-and-a-half big bets per hour, and a win rate of two big bets per hour is considered phenomenal. It's generally easier to achieve a high win rate in low-limit and middle-limit games, where the competition is softest. At the higher limits, win rates drop despite the actual dollars being bigger. To take an example, a professional who can beat a $15/$30 game for 1.5 big bets per hour may be better off there than in a $20/$40 game he can beat for only one big bet per hour.

Protect Yourself with a Bankroll

Let's assume your records confirm that at your current level of stakes, it's plausible you're a winning player. What's the next step in coping with variance?

Simple enough. Essentially, if you play poker for any stakes above nickel-ante, you should set aside a set amount of money dedicated only to playing. In poker terms, this is called a *bankroll*.

Poker experts who are handy with statistics have come up with numbers to describe how big your bankroll should be to avoid going broke. In general, these numbers suggest that if you're playing limit poker and you're a winning player, you should start with a bankroll of 200 to 300 big bets. So for example, if you're playing $3/$6 Hold'em at your local casino, you'd want a bankroll of $1,200 to $1,800 starting out.

This might seem like a lot of money to commit to what is just a hobby—and indeed, many recreational poker players avoid thinking in terms of a bankroll. They just pull money out of their pocket as they go along. But a bankroll is a far better approach. You'll feel more comfortable during losing streaks, and winning streaks won't get you as puffed up. If you have a regular job or other sources of income, you don't literally have to keep your bankroll separate from your other assets. It's enough just to know the amount.

If you encounter the happy problem of an expanding bankroll, you'll have two choices: either pull the money out as profit, or plow it back in. Plowing it back in will eventually allow you to move up to a higher limit, if that's your ambition.

Poker Time Versus Life Time

Just a brief mention here: along with good record-keeping and a bankroll, you should also use plain common sense to keep poker from rattling you. The best antidote for a losing streak is often to take a break. Even when winning, don't focus too much on the game; allow time in your life for family, friends, and other pursuits.

It's important to remember that while poker has a good deal in common with games of skill like chess and bridge, it also shares common elements with roulette, craps, and other gambling games. As such, it can be insidiously addictive. Taking a break can help you keep your perspective—and avoid getting you hooked.

Watch Your Chips

We suggest being especially careful about online poker: its constant availability makes it easy to get over-involved. You may want to set a schedule—for example, play a lot one week, then take the next week off. Or just play on weekends. However you do it, you'll have more fun and less frustration if you keep it fresh.

Turning Pro

This is a long shot, but it may happen: you steadily get better, until you find yourself sitting in middle-limit games and beating them. You've come to rely on the small income you generate from poker to pay for extras like a new computer or a vacation.

If this is the case, you can already regard yourself as a semi-professional player. As long as you keep a good balance, there's no reason you can't keep your day job and have some profitable fun on the side. There's not much more to say about that.

But what if it occurs to you that you enjoy poker *more* than your day job. Why not make it your real job, then? Playing the game you enjoy so much for a living—why not?

There are lots of reasons why not. Here are some of them:

- Remember variance? It's not impossible that you could enjoy several years of excellent results, only to discover you were statistically overachieving. Tales are rife in Las Vegas of technically unsound newcomers who skyrocketed for a year or two, then fizzled as their lack of fundamentals caught up to them.

- As countless pros have found before you, what's fun part-time can be brutal as a daily job. This applies especially to online play. Judging by posts on the online poker forums, legions of college students or recent grads, generally male, are attempting to make a go of it as online poker professionals. Very few will survive; the rest will exhaust themselves, then discover how far behind they've fallen in developing conventional job prospects.

- To succeed at high-stakes poker in particular, you've got to persuade yourself that the big stacks of money you're shoving onto the table are only good for gambling with. This cultivated indifference to money seems to get many big-time pros in trouble, as they periodically go broke or gamble their poker millions away on trivialities like sports betting.

● Think it's hard to get consumer credit as a writer, artist, or freelancer? Just try it if you list your occupation as "poker professional."

It's our opinion (and it's only an opinion) that Hold'em is better as a hobby or even a second job than as a full-time focus. However, we do know full-time professionals who appear to lead successful and fulfilling lives. If you do find yourself winning steadily and can envision making Hold'em a rewarding career, you certainly won't be alone.

The Least You Need to Know

● Keep records of your playing sessions, using hours played, stakes, and wins and losses to calculate your average hourly rate.

● Create a poker bankroll to sustain you through times of hardship and plenty alike. To be safe, aim for a bankroll of 200 to 300 times the big bet at your current limit.

● Be wary of getting too hooked on poker— especially online poker—to the exclusion of other things in life.

● If you ever think about going pro, take a hard look at the potential liabilities and the soundness of your poker skills.

Hold'em Terminology

aggressive   Frequently betting or raising.

all-in   To bet your last remaining chips on a hand, so that you have nothing left. More common in tournaments and in *no-limit* than in *limit*.

angleshooting   Unethical tricks and ploys designed to win the pot or gain an advantage for the angleshooter who uses them.

ante   In poker in general, a bet required of all players before the first card is dealt. Hold'em is usually played with a special form of ante, called *blinds*.

baby   A small card, generally a Six or lower.

baby no-limit   No-limit played for very small stakes, such as $1 to $2 blinds with a maximum $100 buy-in.

backdoor   A draw that requires two consecutive cards to hit. For example, a backdoor flush draw requires additional suited cards on both the turn and the river.

bad beat   An especially stinging defeat. Generally reserved for hands in which you were the presumptive favorite, but your opponent ignored the principles of sound play and got lucky.

bankroll   Money reserved for playing poker. Used by smart players to protect against *variance*.

bicycle   See *wheel*.

big blind   See *blinds*.

Big Slick   Nickname for AK. Also known as "Walking Back to Houston" for its propensity to *bust out* when no Ace or King flops.

blinds   Blind bets required prior to cards being dealt. In *limit* Hold'em, the *little blind* or *small blind* can be from ⅓ to ⅔ the initial bet size, and is *posted* by the player one seat to the left of the *button*; the *big blind* is a full bet, and is posted by the player two seats to the left of the button.

board   The currently displayed *community cards*, whether the flop alone, the flop plus turn, or the flop plus turn and river.

brick and mortar   A casino, club, or other venue where live Hold'em games are offered, as opposed to online play.

bubble   See *on the bubble*.

burn   When dealing either the flop, turn, or river, the dealer first *burns* the top card in the deck by discarding it face-down, and only then deals the common cards. Intended to discourage cheating.

bust out   Of *hole cards*: to lose by failing to connect in any way with the *board*. Of a player in a tournament: to lose all one's chips and be forced to drop out.

button   The marker (usually a plastic disk) that moves left with each deal, denoting the last player to act for that hand. Also shorthand for the player with the button: "The button raised."

buy-in   Chips initially purchased when joining a Hold'em table.

call   To match the amount of a bet.

calling station   A player who habitually calls when he should fold.

cash game   A regular or non-tournament poker game.

check   To take no action when it's your turn to bet. Checking is allowed only in the absence of a bet on the table.

check-raise   To check the first time the action comes to you, then raise if a player behind you bets.

chop   In a casino game, if all players fold to the *blinds*, these two players can agree to chop—meaning each takes back his blind bet rather than play the hand out. This avoids paying the *rake*, which is generally high in low-stakes games and which would be especially onerous in a pot involving only two players.

community cards   Those cards comprising the *flop*, *turn*, and *river*, which are shared by all players.

connected, connectors   *Hole cards* adjacent in rank, such as 98.

counterfeit   If you *flop* or *turn* a *flush* or *straight*, and a card comes on the next *street* which fails to improve your hand but makes possible a higher flush or straight for an opponent, you have been *counterfeited*.

cutoff   A positional term, indicating the player to the immediate right of the player with the dealer *button*.

dealer   The player with the *button*.

dealer button   See *button*.

dominated   If one hand has only three outs against another, that hand is said to be *dominated*. An example is AK and AQ. Excluding straights, the AQ has only the remaining three Queens as *outs* to win. All other cards, including an Ace, favor the AK.

draw   As a noun, a hand such as a straight or a flush; as a verb, to call a bet in hopes of making such a hand on the next card.

drawing hand   See *draw*.

early position   Relative to the dealer *button*, to be one of the first players required to act. Generally a disadvantage.

expectation In poker, a means of examining probabilities to determine whether a given play will make or cost you money in the long run. The former is *positive expectation*, the latter, *negative expectation*.

fish A weak, losing player.

floor A general term for cardroom managers.

flop The first three common cards, followed by the *turn* and the *river*.

flush A five-card poker hand in which all five cards are of the same suit.

fold To decline to call a bet or raise by discarding your cards.

full house A five-card poker hand comprised of three-of-a-kind plus a pair.

get broke To lose all your chips in a no-limit game. Also see *bust out*.

good game A game in which you can expect to make money from one or more very bad players.

hand Used variously to mean either your hole cards, any five-card combination of your *hole cards* and the *community cards*, or any given deal of the cards.

head-up, heads-up A hand limited to two players.

hole cards The two private face-down cards held by every player. Also called *pocket* cards.

hourly rate   The average amount you make (or lose) for each hour of play. Usually measured both in dollars and in big bets for a given *limit*.

implied odds   A variation of *pot odds*, in which calling a relatively small bet with a drawing hand gives you a chance of making that hand and collecting future bets of greater size.

jam   To put in the maximum raises on any given *street*.

kicker   If you pair one of your hole cards with a card on the *board*, your unpaired card is your kicker.

late position   To be either the *dealer* or nearly so, and thus among the last to act on each betting round. Generally an advantage.

leak   A flaw in your game that reduces your *expectation*.

limit   Poker in which bets and raises are limited to a preset amount. Also refers to a given level of stakes. See also *no-limit* and *pot-limit*.

limp   To play hole cards before the flop by calling the *big blind*, rather than raising.

little blind   See *blinds*.

loose   To play too many hands, call too many raises, and so on.

loose-aggressive   A loose player who loves to bet and loves raising even more.

loose-passive   A loose player who hates to bet and hates raising even more.

made hand   The opposite of a drawing hand; a hand that doesn't need to improve to be a possible winner. Examples include big *pocket* pairs and high pairs made by pairing the *board*.

mathematical expectation   See *expectation*.

middle position   Relative to the dealer *button*, to be among neither the first nor the last players required to act.

muck   To fold hole cards by discarding them face down in the direction of the dealer. Also a noun referring to the existing heap of discarded cards.

negative expectation   See *expectation*.

no-limit   Poker in which no limit is placed on the size of raises or bets, up to the amount of chips or cash a player has on the table.

nuts   The best possible hand as determined by the *community cards*. Note that each new community card can redefine the nuts.

odds   A ratio expressing the chances of a desired event occurring. In the case of poker, this event is either winning the pot (with no more cards to come) or drawing a card that improves your hand to the winner (with exactly one card to come). See also *pot odds*, *implied odds*, *reverse implied odds*, and *outs*.

offsuit   Unsuited hole cards.

on the bubble   In tournaments, players struggling to keep from getting eliminated and who are only a slot or two away from sharing in the prize money are said to be *on the bubble*.

open   To begin the betting on a particular *street*.

open-ended   A straight draw with eight outs, the maximum. An example would be holding hole cards of JT on a flop of 98x: any of the four Sevens or four Queens would make a straight.

outs   Cards that can improve your hand on the turn or the river.

overbet   In *no-limit*, to bet an amount larger than the pot.

overcards   Hole cards higher in rank than any *community cards*.

passive   Rarely betting or raising. Generally a losing approach in poker.

play back   To respond aggressively to a bet or raise by raising back in return.

pocket   See *hole cards*.

position   Your seat relative to the *button*. In Hold'em, position determines who acts first. All things being equal, the later your position, the more information you have and the greater your advantage over players who must act before you.

positive expectation   See *expectation*.

post   To make a blind bet; for example, "He posted the *big blind*."

pot-limit   Poker in which bets and raises are limited to the size of the pot. This allows the pot to grow geometrically.

pot odds   In poker, the ratio of the pot you hope to win versus the total bet you must call. Usually compared to odds.

preflop   Shorthand for all action occurring before the *flop*.

quads   Four-of-a-kind, such as KKKK.

raise   As a verb, to bet an additional amount over and above the current bet; as a noun, a bet that increases the current bet.

rake   The portion of a pot taken by the casino as its way of making money from a poker game.

redraw   The possibility of improving a strong made hand by catching a card that makes it even stronger, and thus beating a drawing hand that had temporarily improved to beat you.

reverse implied odds   A situation wherein you flop a made hand such as top pair, but face many opponents with good drawing hands. Most of the cards that can come will help them and do nothing for you, so your chances of winning only get worse.

ring game   Any game with seven or more players. Most Hold'em advice pertains to ring games, as opposed to *short-handed* games.

river   The fifth and final *community card*.

run over   To win money from a timid opponent by playing extra-aggressively, often with bluffs and unorthodox raises.

second pair   The second-highest pair on a particular flop or board.

semi-bluff   To bet or raise with a drawing hand in hopes that your opponent may fold, knowing that even if he doesn't, you may still win if your hand improves.

set   Three-of-a-kind made by holding a pocket pair which matches one community card. See also *trips*.

short-handed   Any game with six or fewer players. Short-handed games require a different strategy than *ring games*.

showdown   The revealing of players' hands after all betting has been concluded on the river. Only required if more than one player is still in.

small blind   See *blinds*.

spread limit   A form of *limit* poker in which bets may be any amount between a stated minimum and maximum. Raises must be at least the amount of the previous bet. For example, if a player makes an initial bet of $2, you can raise to make the total bet anywhere from $4 to $5 ($4 plus $4, or $4 plus $3), but not $3 ($2 plus $1).

stack   The amount of chips a player has in front of him or her.

straddle   A blind raise allowed by most casinos and clubs in which the *under-the-gun* player posts a raise before the cards are dealt.

straight   A five-card poker hand in which all five cards are consecutive in rank.

street   The current betting round. In Hold'em, the streets are *preflop*, *flop*, *turn*, and *river*.

structured limit   A form of *limit* poker in which bets and raises must be a fixed amount. For Hold'em, the limit typically doubles on the turn. Common structured limits are $2/$4, $3/$6, $5/$10, $10/$20, and so on.

suited   Two *hole cards* of the same suit.

suited trash   Suited hole cards too far apart in rank to make a straight—for example, J3s or 92s.

tainted outs   Cards dealt during the *flop*, *turn*, or *river* that can improve your hand, but may improve an opponent's hand more. For example, if you have a straight draw and an opponent has a flush draw, two of your outs will be of his suit and thus tainted. See also *outs*.

tell   An unintentional physical betrayal by a player regarding the quality of his hand or his intentions. Includes mannerisms, tone of voice, posture, facial expressions, and so on.

tight   The opposite of loose: a player who folds most of his hole cards, calls few raises, and so on.

tilt   To play badly when upset or angry; often occurs after a *bad beat*.

top pair   The best pair made possible by the current *board*.

trash hand   A hand of such irredeemably low quality that it should generally be folded rather than played.

trips   Three-of-a-kind. In Hold'em, this generally refers to three-of-a-kind made with one of your hole cards and two *community cards*.

turn   The fourth *community card*, coming after the flop and before the river.

two pair   A five-card poker hand made up of two different pairs and an unrelated card.

under-the-gun   Before the flop, this is the first player to act—that is, the first player seated to the left of the blinds.

variance   The semi-random fluctuations in a poker player's wins and losses over time.

weak-tight   Prone to folding all but the very best hands.

wheel   The smallest possible straight, from Ace through Five, with the Ace counting as a low card rather than a high card.

Hold'em Odds Tables

The following tables assume you're familiar with the concepts of drawing odds and counting your outs, in the form of cards that can improve your hand. If you need to, review Chapter 3.

Odds for Flopping Good with Various Hole Cards

These odds are interesting, but not vital to memorize. It's worth noting that the odds of flopping a straight draw, flush draw, or set are considerably worse than the odds of flopping a pair when holding two big cards. This is one reason why you want more company with drawing hands such as small pairs and suited connectors.

Note also that we didn't list the full range of possibilities. For example, if you hold AK, there are many additional hands you can flop that are better than a single pair—two pair, a straight, a full house, a backdoor flush draw, and so on.

Odds for Flopping Good with Various Hole Cards

Hand	Example	Desired Hand	Percent	Odds Against
Pocket pair	AA	Set	10.8%	8.3 to 1
Big cards	AK	Pair	29%	2.5 to 1
Suited cards	A3s	Flush draw	11%	8.1 to 1
Offsuit connectors	98	Straight draw	11.8%	7.5 to 1
Suited connectors	JTs	Straight or flush draw	16%	5 to 1

Two Pair

Odds from Flop to Turn

What are the chances your hand will improve on the flop by seeing one more card—namely, the turn?

To read this table, first count your outs in the left column before looking at your percent change of improving and the odds against doing so. Note that although we include percentages for the sake of completeness, in practice you'll think mostly in terms of odds and outs.

12

Odds from Flop to Turn

Outs	Percent	Odds to 1	Example
15	31.9	2.1	Straight flush draw, drawing to either a straight or a flush
14	29.8	2.4	
13	27.7	2.6	
12	25.5	2.9	
11	23.4	3.3	
10	21.3	3.7	Set, drawing to a full house or quads
9	19.1	4.2	Flush draw
8	17.0	4.9	Straight draw
7	14.9	5.7	
6	12.8	6.8	Straight draw vs. flush draw; also over-cards, drawing to top pair
5	10.6	8.4	Pair using board drawing to trips or card, two pair
4	8.5	10.8	Inside straight draw; also two pair, drawing to a full house
3	6.4	14.7	
2	4.3	22.5	Pocket pair, drawing to a set

Odds from Turn to River

Again, you're seeing just one card here, but this time it's the river card. These odds are almost identical to the odds for drawing one card on the flop, so if you want to, you can just remember one set of odds or the other.

Odds from Turn to River

Outs	Percent	Odds to 1	Example
15	32.6	2.1	Straight flush draw, drawing to either a straight or a flush
14	30.4	2.4	
13	28.3	2.5	
12	26.1	2.8	
11	23.9	3.2	
10	21.7	3.6	Set, drawing to a full house or quads
9	19.6	4.1	Flush draw
8	17.4	4.8	Straight draw
7	15.2	5.6	
6	13.0	6.7	Straight draw vs. flush draw; also overcards, drawing to top pair
5	10.9	8.2	Pair using board card, drawing to trips or two pair

Outs	Percent	Odds to 1	Example
4	8.7	10.5	Inside straight draw; also two pair, drawing to a full house
3	6.5	14.3	
2	4.3	22.0	Pocket pair, drawing to a set

Odds from Flop to River

Let's say you plan to see *both* the turn and the river in your quest to improve.

You're seeing two cards rather than just one—so shouldn't your odds be twice as good? In fact, they're not. The answer is complicated from a mathematical standpoint, but you can take our word for it that the following table reflects your true percentages and odds for a two-card draw.

Odds from Flop to River

Outs	Percent	Odds to 1	Example
15	54.1	0.8*	Straight flush draw, drawing to either a straight or a flush
14	51.2	1.0	
13	48.1	1.1	
12	45.0	1.2	

continues

Odds from Flop to River (continued)

Outs	Percent	Odds to 1	Example
11	41.7	1.4	
10	38.4	1.6	Set, drawing to a full house or quads
9	35.0	1.9	Nut flush draw
8	31.5	2.2	Straight draw
7	27.8	2.6	
6	24.1	3.1	Straight draw vs. flush draw; also overcards, drawing to top pair
5	20.3	3.9	Pair using board card, drawing to trips or two pair
4	16.5	5.1	Inside straight draw; also two pair, drawing to a full house
3	12.5	7.0	
2	8.4	10.9	Pocket pair, drawing to a set

You're a 1.2 to 1 favorite.

Race Odds When Head-Up and All-In

For no-limit, it's good to know the odds of one type of hand versus another when two players have gone all-in before the flop. This table shows some common scenarios.

Race Odds When Head-Up and All-In

Category	Example	Race Odds
Higher pair vs. lower pair	K♠K♥ Q♠Q♦	Higher pair is 4.5 to 1 favorite
Smaller pair vs. two high cards	9♥9♣ A♠K♦	Smaller pair is 6 to 5 favorite
Higher pair vs. small suited connectors	T♠T♦ 6♣5♣	Pair is 3.5 to 1 favorite
Higher pair vs. unsuited smaller cards	J♣J♥ 7♣5♦	Pair is 5 to 1 favorite
Pair vs. higher and lower card	8♥8♣ A♦6♥	Pair is 5 to 2 favorite
Two higher cards vs. two lower cards	A♦Q♣ T♣9♥	Higher cards are 5 to 3 favorite

Flush $\frac{13}{52}$ 11   3

$$5 \cdot \frac{11}{52} \cdot \frac{10}{49} \cdot \frac{9}{48} = \frac{99}{2352} = 4.2\%$$

-2 in pocket

<u>Opp</u>   <u>Drawn</u>   <u>No</u>

~~NN~~ ~~NN~~   11   ~~NN~~ ~~NN~~ ~~NN~~
~~NN~~ ~~NN~~ 11   ~~NN~~

Poker Resources

After you've read the covers off this book and played a few hundred hours of Hold'em, you'll be ready for more advanced information. Toward that end, here are some books, online resources, and software to help you hone your skills.

Recommended Books

Brunson, Doyle. *Doyle Brunson's Super System.* Cardoza Publishing, 1979.

One of the most venerated poker books of all time, now available in paperback. Much of the advice has been rendered out-of-date, but the no-limit Hold'em section is still required reading if that's your game.

Burgess, Randy, with Carl Baldassarre. *The Ultimate Guide to Poker Tells: Devastate Opponents by Reading Body Language, Table Talk, Chip Moves, and Much More.* Triumph Books, 2006.

Like live play? Then you'll love learning how to read opponents' hands through tells. The early chapters of this book dispel various misconceptions about the subject; later chapters walk you through specific tells for both limit and no-limit Hold'em. It even includes photos.

Burgess, Randy. *Stepping Up: The Recreational Player's Guide to Beating Casino and Internet Poker*. ConJelCo, 2003.

If you've played a lot of home poker but are still hesitant about setting foot in a casino, this is the book for you. Included are chapters on reading players and hands in Hold'em, avoiding strategic mistakes, taming tilt, and refining your game.

Ciaffone, Bob, and Stewart Reuben. *Pot-Limit and No-Limit Poker*. Bob Ciaffone, 1999.

This book presents the clearest explanation available of basic concepts in making the transition from limit to no-limit Hold'em. Every beginning no-limit player should read this book.

Cooke, Roy, and John Bond. *Real Poker: The Cooke Collection*. Mike Caro University, 1999.

A collection of columns originally written for *Card Player Magazine*. Roy Cooke is one of those rare poker writers who admits to being human and making mistakes; on the other hand, he's a heck of a good Hold'em player. The combination makes this book both entertaining and highly instructive.

Harrington, Dan, and Bill Robertie. *Harrington on Hold'em, Volume 1 and Volume 2*. Two Plus Two Publishing, 2004, 2005.

This two-volume set represents a considerable advance over previous books on no-limit tournament Hold'em. It's meant for intermediate players, so you'll want to gain a fair amount of tournament experience before delving in.

Miller, Ed. *Small Stakes Hold'em: Winning Big with Expert Play*. Two Plus Two Publishing, 2004.

A fabulous advance in the literature of Hold'em, concentrating on beating loose games full of terrible opponents. The only down side is that Miller is writing well over the heads of beginners. But that's no excuse for not reading this book after you've got more experience.

Sklansky, David. *The Theory of Poker*. Two Plus Two Publishing, 1989.

If you want a deeper understanding of poker in general, including but not limited to Hold'em, this is the best book out there. Just be prepared to put in some serious study time!

Online Forums

Hands down, www.twoplustwo.com is the best poker forum online; the discussions are lively and many of the posters are top-notch. Just be prepared for brutal honesty: your fellow posters won't hold back when educating you about your mistakes.

Software

StatKing is a handy Windows program for keeping track of your poker results and calculating such neat stuff as your hourly rate and standard deviation (a measure of how big your swings are). It's available from ConJelCo, at www.conjelco.com.

If you only play online, you may want to skip StatKing and use PokerTracker instead. This program gets rave reviews from online players for its ability to import hand histories from most of the popular online sites and instantly presents you with statistics not only for your own play, but for opponents as well. A free demo is available from www.pokertracker.com.

Wilson Software makes a variety of widely respected poker practice programs, including one for Hold'em called Turbo Texas Hold'em. Although the initial price of around $90 may seem steep, it's a great way to get practice without losing money at the tables. See www.wilsonsoftware.com for more information.

Index

W-X-Y-Z